CAPPADOCIA

By
Jeoffrey Lamec

CONTENTS:

THE FORMATION

A view of Hasan Mountain
Uçhisar, landscape of tufa formations (left)

Millions of years ago, during the 3rd. geological period, Mid-Anatolian Plateau was an inner sea surrounded by forests and plains, which were not higher than 500 meters. Characteristic animals of the time, such as Nummilit, Mastadon and Hipparion, were living in the region. In the south, between Lycaonia(northeast of Konya) and the Taurus Mountains range, a series of volcanoes appeared as a result of the movement of the Taurus Mountains. Between Erciyes Mountain(Argeus/3,917m), which is southwest of Kayseri and Karacadağ, several beautiful cone-shaped mountains, such as Dede Mountain, Melendiz Mountains(2,935m), Göllü Mountain(2,143m) north of Nenezi, Grand Hasan Mountain(Athar/3,268m) and Little Hasan Mountain became volcanically active. The continuous eruptions of these mountains have structured Mid-Anatolian Plateau with masses of lava and ash that are 200 meters in height. This volcanic activity has lasted until the present Halosen Era. It is believed that Hipparion, which is an ancestor of the modern horse, went extinct because of the volcanic eruptions. Based on examinations of the fossils from

Erciyes Mountain (Erciyes Volcano)(top).
Göreme, Landscape of tufa cones from Kılıçlar Valley (left).

both Taşkınpaşa Village and the hills around Kızılasma Valley, it is assumed that these animals went extinct 10 million years ago during the late Miocene Age. In the 4th. geological time (two million years ago), the earth went through climatic changes that included four different ice ages like, Gunz, Mindell, Riss and Wurm. Although there are traces of civilizations from the Paleolithic Age but these traces do not go back earlier than late Paleolithic. It is believed that the long-lasting presence of glaciers from the Wurm ice age in Asia Minor is the reason that civilizations did not inhabit this region. Moreover, continuous volcanic eruptions made the situation even worse.

With the end of the ice ages the climate became milder and in Cappadocia, especially around Konya and Aksaray, several lakes appeared. Ash, sandstone, clay, basalt and ignimbrite, soft tufa and other minerals that make up the volcanic layers eroded by natural forces and formed the unique rock formations that are only seen in Cappadocia. Soft tufa stones and basalt layers were affected differently by the erosion process. Interesting canyons and the well-known **Cappadocian Fairy Chimneys** appeared as a result of this process.

In the region, there are rivers with continuous and ample water flow like Kızılırmak has an indispensable role in the drainage of melting snow. Another river, Melendiz, has a lot of water resources. Valleys that had a good water supply provided inhabitants of the area with the necessary life resources to survive.

High rocky hills around the valleys gave a safe shelter from outside dangers. Soft tufa rock could be shaped without even the use of metals and were used by the civilizations of the area.

Uçhisar, Tufa cones with rock dwellings (left) and Fairy chimneys of Ürgüp (up).

Prehistoric Evidences in Cappadocia

For hundreds of thousands of years, human populations survived by hunting, fishing and collecting fruits or plant roots. They settled near lakes or rivers because of their dependence on water for survival. A river like Kızılırmak with its broad banks and fertile surrounding hills has been an ideal habitat for Anatolian people. Natural disasters, wars and continuous restructuring make it very difficult to trace older civilizations. It is difficult to trace the early civilizations of the area. Sometimes, however, it is possible to find clues that change our understanding of history by means of excavations. Konya plain was a lake until 16,000-8,000 B.C.. While the ice age still existed in western Europe a mild, humid climate became dominant in Anatolia. There were a lot pastures, making the Konya plain very suitable for raising animals, and there was ample, fertile land abounding in water for agriculture. Pastures and swamps laid to east, while salty swamps laid to the north. Climatic changes that started 12,000 years ago dried up the lakes in middle Anatolia. The Konya and Aksaray Plains and Lake Salt(Tuz Gölü) were formed in this era. The biggest transformation in world history started in Anatolia. Hunting, which had existed since the ice ages, was replaced with agriculture in open areas without thick forests. Human groups started to live in a certain area permanently. For the first time in human history they started to found religions. Humankind was exploring and enjoying the opportunities of a settled life thanks to a new friendship with soil. This was a challenging, yet holy, endeavor.

Researching of the Neolithic times in Anatolia is quite new. English archaeologists found stone gadgets from the Paleolithic and Neolithic times on Avla hill, which is 8 km southeast of Ürgüp. Similarly, research done by the Ankara English Archaeology Institute between 1964-1966 revealed interesting information about the area.

As a result of this research done on the surface layers of the earth led by Ian Todd, many inhabitances, most of which were in Nevşehir and Niğde, were uncovered. Inhabitances such as Iğdeli Çeşme, in Nevşehir, Acıgöl, and the one in Tatlarin, are some of the examples of sites of the Neolithic era.

An Illustration of Çatalhöyük houses (after James Melaart's drawing) (upper left).
Mother Goddess (Kybele) of Çatalhöyük (left). Deer hunting. An illustration from the original Çatalhöyük fresco (up).

Çatalhöyük

In 1956 it was assumed that in most of Turkey, and especially in Anatolia, it wouldn't be possible to find any inhabitances from the **Neolithic era**. Neolithic cultures are classified in two major groups: Aceramic (without pottery) and Ceramic (with pottery). In 1961 the biggest inhabitance from the Neolithic era, Çatalhöyük, was found 15km south-east of Konya. The discovery of Çatalhöyük is significant because it was the first sign to show that there were relics from the Neolithic era (7,100-6,300 B. C.) in Anatolia. Excavation was done in the area by **James Mellaart** between 1961-1965. Since 1993, an international archaeological team led by Professor Ian Hodder has done excavation and research in the area. In a typical **Çatalhöyük house**, heating and cooking were done by means of a fireplace. Holes under the houses were used to put stone tombs, extra rooms, or symbols that showed the fertility of the clan. Painting was used to decorate the walls with themes about hunting and funeral ceremonies. The most interesting of these frescoes had two erupting volcanic mountains in the background, which are assumed to be Büyük Hasan and Küçük Hasan Mountains, with the inhabitance of Çatalhöyük in the foreground. In fact, you can actually see the zenith of the Hasan Mountains from Çatalhöyük on clear days. This fresco was the first city plan of Çatalhöyük. It also shows us the enormous influence of volcanic mountains on people's lives. In the beginning, Çatalhöyük was situated in

Çatalhöyük fresco. The settlement of a village in front and an active Volcano(Hasan Dağ) in the background can be seen (illustration from the original fresco).

an area composed of pastures and fertile agricultural land abounding in water. There were a lot of wild animals in the surrounding area. People of Çatalhöyük lived in the very same area for 900 years. Artifacts found from this time are fascinating. Fabrics were produced using plant fibers and animal hair that were sewn using bone needles. Leather garments and fur coats are only a couple of examples of the articles of clothing found. Leopard skins assumed to have been used during ceremonies, lead and copper wire that are among the first examples of metal crafting, beads, needles, statues of **Mother Goddess** and the first ***obsidian*** mirrors of the world are other examples of the findings at this site. Çarşamba stream, which flows from the Toros Mountains, divided Çatalhöyük into two. Between 6,300-5,700 B.C., for some unknown reason, people left their old inhabitance and moved into west Çatalhöyük, which is on the other side of the Çarşamba stream (late Neolithic era). During the same time, there were similar movements in the other Neolithic inhabitances in the area. This was the beginning of a new era in Anatolia the Kalkolithic age/period/era (5,900-3,200 B.C.) During the Kalkolithic era, doors that opened to the garden were used instead of entrances from the ceiling. These kinds of houses are the first examples of "Megaron"-type buildings that have been used in Anatolia for thousands of years. The dead were buried in cemeteries outside of the house instead of within the house. The number of **Mother Goddess** figures, which symbolized fertility, increased. Villages turned into towns, plows were used in agriculture, the number of domestic animals increased, and pottery production evolved into an artistic form during the Kalkolithic era.

Aşıklı Höyük and Musular

Aşıklı Höyük is 25km southeast of the modern city of Aksaray, 1.5km south of the village of Kızılkaya, in the borders of the town of Gülağaç. The inhabitance of Aşıklı Höyük was founded in the Cappadocia region on volcanic land that is in a bowl-shaped area surrounded by the Hasan Mountains and Melendiz Mountain range. It is on the north side of the Ihlara Valley near Melendiz stream. It is 230 meters east to west and 150 meters north to south. It is from the Aceramic Neolithic era. The Mamasın Dam is going to cover most of the tumulus with water when its construction ends therefore, since 1989, a research team from the Prehistory department of the University of İstanbul, led by Prof. Dr.Ufuk ESİN, has been excavating to save it. It is one of the first villages from the Anatolian and Near Eastern **Aceramic Neolithic era**. It has two cultural layers. Houses that are made from adobe are separated from each other by narrow roads.

The entrances to the houses were on the roof and long ladders were used to go up to the roof since there were no doors that opened into the narrow roads. The floor and the walls were covered with mud or pebbles. There were stoves in the walls covered with pebbles. The inhabitance is divided into two with a pebbly road. On the other side of the road there was a temple painted the color red ocher with a lean-to annex. Relics of a massive wall made of stone were found surrounding the village. Also found were many half-crafted obsidian stones. Some of the skeletons had copper beads around their necks, which shows us that copper was processed in these old times.

Musular is a kilometer south of the village of Kızılkaya, in the borders of the town of Gülağaç. Heading south after the Güzelyurt and Ihlara exit on the route from Aksaray to Nevşehir, it is 18km. It is in the middle of an agricultural land directly west of Aşıklı Höyük. In 1996, Prof.Dr.Ufuk ESİN and his team found the bones of many cattle and wild horses, obsidian arrow heads, chiseled stone tools used to shape animal bones, obsidian tools, and ornaments made from agate and various other stones. The houses are from the late **Aceramic Neolithic era** (7,000 B.C.), when people of the area used to have large hunting ceremonies and lived on agriculture and cattle-raising. Horses started to be tamed during this time.

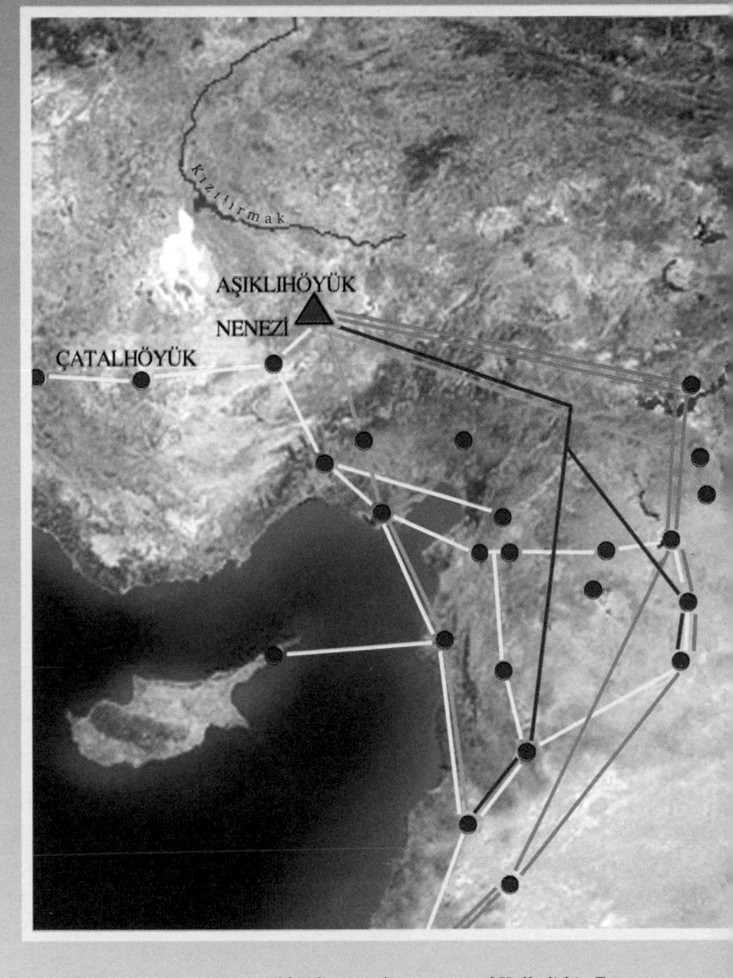

Obsidian trading routes of Kalkolithic Era.

NENEZİ

Nenezi was first found during excavations by S. Payne in the Nevşehir-Niğde area. Pieces of obsidian that Payne found in the east of the village of Bekarlar, in the borders of Aksaray on the west side of Nenezi Mountain, as well as the remnants of an obsidian mine on the flat area near the mountain, made Payne think that this might have been an

Excavations in Aşıklı Höyük (top). A rock-dwelling grave at Göreme from the Roman period (right)..

obsidian-processing place. In the same place between 1993-1999 N. Balkan ATLI, from the Istanbul University department of prehistory, researched, and his findings led other researchers to conclude that a Nenezi Mountain obsidian workshop processed obsidian blocks and that the products were exported. In these workshops obsidian was first mined and half-processed to be sold or bartered, not only the local inhabitances, but also to far-off places such as Eriha in Jordan. The results of examinations of the obsidian tools found in Aşıklı Höyük in 1999 indicates that they are from Göllü Mountain and Nenezi Mountain and they were produced in the **Aceramic Neolithic** era.

Güvercin Kayası

The artifacts found during the excavations, led by the city museum of Aksaray, parallel those found in Çatalhöyük and Alişarhöyük. During the excavations, aside from **Neolithic** and **Kalkolithic** pieces that can be categorized as tools and weapons made mainly from copper, cutting and piercing tools made of bones that were probably related to fishing. This helped the researchers to find an 8,000 year old fishermen's village in the area that was covered with little lakes at the time. The village had one-room houses with very narrow streets. It is likely that ceramic items found will shed light onto the yet unknown Middle Anatolia **Kalkolithic** period.

Cuneiform Inscription of Kadesh Pact between Hittites and Egyptians (top) and a sample of Cappadocian Tablets (Archeological Museum of Istanbul)(bottom).

Towards the end of the 4th century B.C. and in the early years of the 3rd century, the use of copper and tin in different parts of daily life started the Old Bronze Age in Anatolia.

Metal and gold objects and ornaments found in the excavations of Acemhöyük shed light on our knowledge about this age in Anatolia. Heinrich Schliemann couldn't know that the Troy treasure that he found while looking for the legendary city of Homer stemmed from the second part of the Old Bronze Age in Anatolia..

HISTORICAL ACCOUNT

Hittite chariot (Late Hittite Period. Museum of the Anatolian Civilizations-Ankara).

The primary way to learn about the history of societies in a geographical area is to examine the written sources from the past. No kind of writing existed in Anatolia before the beginning of the 2nd century B.C.. Between XX. and XVIII. c B.C. Assyrian traders founded commercial colonies in Anatolia called karums. Kaniş (Kültepe) in Cappadocia was one of these colonies. Thanks to the commercial registers of the local principalities the first written documents in Anatolia, called the **Cuiciform Tablets of Cappadocia**, were created. Until the kingdom of the Hittites was founded in 1700 B.C. no political documents or documents related to daily life were created. Hittites blended very well with the local culture, even adopting their language and religion, since they moved from Caucasia to Anatolia over a long period of time. In the New Bronze Age, the borders of the Hittite kingdom were from Kültepe (east of the modern city of Ankara) to Boğazköy, to Troy in western Anatolia, to Afyon and even to Lykia(Lukka), including all of Cappadocia. The most significant gods of the Hittites are the god of the storm, Teşup, originating from

Hatti-Hurri, and his wife Hepat. In the depictions Hepat is shown on a lion and Teşup is shown stepping on the backs of two mountain gods that were drawn into the shape of humans. These mountains, **Namni** and **Hazzi**, are most likely the mountains of Erciyes and Hasan. One of the legends tells about the time when the god of the storm was angry and caused a terrible disaster that filled the houses with fog and smoke, made the fields barren, and destroyed pastures and other natural sources. It is probable that this story is related to a legendary volcanic change in Anatolia. The same legend tells us that life returned back to normal after a period of time. Hittite inscriptions, often accompanied by stone reliefs, can be found in Yazılıkaya open-air temple near Boğazköy in Hattuşa on Hasan and Göllü Mountains. It is acknowledged that it is Hittites who founded the castles in Aksaray, Selime and Toprakhisar. A lot of names that are used for cities and geographical regions originated from **Hatti, Luwi** and **Hittite**. Moreover, Neşa (Nyssa), a language unique to Cappadocia, is actually the Hittite language.

With the end of the Assyrian trade colonies in Anatolia, Kültepe and Kaniş lost their significance. Since **Hattusha** became the capital city of the state, northern parts of the Anatolian Plateau became more important. With the downfall of the Hittite kingdom, (1200 BC) the tradition of writing ceased as well. Egyptian sources mention that sea tribes marched into their country in big groups on ox carts, and none of the cities could stand against this enormous power. Eventually, Egypt was able to keep these sea tribes away from its borders. However, all relationships with Anatolia came to an end. After the great Hittite kingdom, the second biggest state that we know of in Anatolia was the Phrygia kingdom, which was founded in 750 B.C.. From the downfall of the Hittites to the appearance of the Phrygia kingdom, there was a period of 450 years that we can call **the dark age** of Cappadocia. The excavations in Boğazköy indicate that the city was mostly destroyed after a fire and was not inhabited by anybody for a century. As a result, the area around the river **Kızılırmak** was sparsely populated during this period. We know about southeastern Anatolia thanks to the Assyrian sources, as the region was ruled by them starting from the 5th century B.C.. Assyrians constituted a great danger for Hittites, however they were never able to take over the Hittite territory as a result of their own internal problems. Assyrian sources (1st Tiglatpleser Inscriptions) tell us about a 20,000 soldier **Mushki** army commanded by five kings. The name **Mushki** was used for Phrygians in Assyrian sources. The chaos created by the migration after the collapse of the big power lasted a few years. Lydia in the west and Urartu in the east appeared as two new states. Then, in middle and southeast Anatolia **The Late**

A rock relief at İvriz (left),
Yazılıkaya, relief of Hittite Gods in ritueliccеremony (top).
and an inscription from Hittites (Aksaray Museum)(right).

Hittite states appeared. These were called the kingdom of Tabal (700 B.C.), and Kayseri, Niğde, Nevşehir, Aksaray and Ürgüp were within its borders. The capital of this kingdom was **Tuwanuwaa** (Tyana/todays Nigde), Gülşehir, Acıgöl and Hacıbektaş have Hittite stone inscriptions from this era. Kimmerians, who came from north, put end to the reign of Phrygians. To avoid Kimmer attacks Phrygians built numerous castles by chiseling rocks. From this time on, Medians (585 B.C.) and Persians (547 B.C.) habited Anatolia. Persians stayed in Cappadocia until 332 B.C. and ruled the area by dividing it into governorships that they called **Satraps**. Famous **The King Road** was built in this era. The great Alexander, who wiped out Persian Empire in Anatolia, encountered a strong resistance in Cap-

Sarchopagus reliefs of Alexander the Great shows a battle with Persians (Archeological Museum of İstanbul)(top).
The Ihlara (Peristrema) Canyon (left).

padocia (332 -322 B.C.). Actually, in order not to waste time in his other endeavors, Alexander only asked for yearly tax instead of invading the area. Persian governorships came together as an autonomous kingdom that they named **The Cappadocian Kingdom**. They always remained as the main power of Cappadocia (535-332 B.C.), although they disunited or cooperated with other powers from time to time. After the death of Alexander the Great, Cappadocia became one of the states of Roman Empire in 17 B.C.. Before that, the people of Cappadocia lived freely in princedoms far from the world's attention. In 17 B.C. the whole of Cappadocia, like the other regions of Asia Minor, was taken over by Romans. Roman authorities, not paying attention to the influence of Hellenism on people, cared only about keeping significant military and commercial roads. During these times the people of Cappadocia chiseled rocks in order to create hiding places from the Roman tax collectors. During the reign of Emperor Septimus Severus (born in Caeserea/Kayseri today) economical revival occurred. First, Christians of Anatolia built monasteries and churches out of sight in Ihlara and Göreme in 4th century by making use of the soft tufa rocks. During this time, Aksaray and Kayseri turned into important religious centers. Until the end of the 11th century Cappadocia was under the control of Byzantium Empire. Arabians and Sassanis attacked the region during Byzantium reign, and eventually Ottomans took control of the area after the Seljuk Turcs.

According to famous ancient Historian **Herodotos** (born in Halikarnassos-Anatolia), the borders of the Hittite kingdom were the river Firat and Meliten (todays Malatya) in the east, Salt Lake and Lykaonia (todays Konya) in the west, Pontus (The Black Sea) in the north, and the Toros Mountain range in the south. This area was also home to the **Holy Mother Goddess**. Luwi's, who are local to Anatolia, also used horses.

THE NAME "CAPPADOCIA"

*M*any sources mentions that, the name **Katpatuka**, which was in one of the inscriptions of the Persian King Dareios, means **The land of beautiful horses.** Cappadocia was known with the name Katpatuka during the Persian rule in the area. However, there is no agreement about the origins of the word **Katpatuka**, so it might be a Hellenic, Persian, Hatti, Luwi, or Assyrian word. When Hittites, who were nomadic at the beginning, came into Anatolia from Caucasians on horseback, Anatolian people had already settled down, raising cattle, cultivating the land, and even trading. Horses had been being used in Anatolia since very old times. As we mentioned earlier, **Hipparion**, which is known to be the ancestor of todays horse, was living in Anatolia before it went extinct as a result of the volcanic eruptions of the Erciyes, Hasan, and Göllü Mountains in late **Miocene** period.

It is accepted that horses were first tamed by Hurries in the north of Mesopotamia and that the Hellenes and Cretians. Crete learned how to tame horses from them. We learned that Hittites took raising and taming horses very seriously, and they brought specialists to their country from the **Mittani** and **Hurri** kingdoms, from a book that was found in Boğazkoy, and that was written by a young Mittani horse keeper named Kikkuli, about how to raise a horse.

In 1,000 B.C., Anatolian languages originated from **Luwi/Pelasg**. In Luwi language, horse meant **asu**/asuwa and horseman is **Asu-wari**. The word **suvari** (horseman), which has the same meaning in Persian and Turkish today, also originates from the Luwi word . According to Herzfeld, the suffix **uka**, which is at the end of the word **Katpat-uka** is the Med version of the suffix **ukh**, which was used to create nouns that refer to people of a country in Hurri and Luwi languages. Therefore, the word **Katpat-ukh** means homeland of the **Katpat people**. In Anatolia, between 2.000 B.C. and 1.000 B.C., **Hepa**/Hepat known as the **Mother Goddess** and she was considered holy. In the Hurri language she was called **Kuta-Khepat**, which means **Holy Mother Goddess**, the word Katpatuka might also come from **Kuta-Khepat-ukh**, which means **the people of/the Holy Hepa Land**.

In Persian, the phrase **beautiful horse** used as **Huv-aspa**. **Aspa** means horse (Christian Bartholomae–Altiranisches Worterbuch). The word Katpatuka might have been changed into **Kappadocia** in Hellenic pronounciation. In the Hellenic language, the same phrase means **Eu-hippos** or **Euhippe**, and the word **Hipparion** is also of Hellenic origin.

To conclude, whatever the meanings of the words are, in regions of Cappadocia that are not touristy, fine horses certainly have been raised from the time of the Luwis to the Hittites and from the Persians to the Romans. There is something else that is certain; the people of Cappadocia, having worshipped Mother Goddess for thousands of years, embraced the Virgin Mary and her Son and, despite violence and oppression, Christianity grew in Anatolia and spread to the rest of the world from here. All these monuments of Christianity that can be seen and told about today provide us with a good proof of this.

THE SPREAD OF CHRISTIANITY IN CAPPADOCIA

"And on this rock I will build my church, and the gates of Hades will not overcome it. I will give you the keys of the kingdom of heaven; whatever you bind on earth will be bound in heaven, and whatever you loose on earth will be loosed in heaven." (Matthew 16:18-19)

The first church was carved in the rocks of Antakya, inspired by this Bible passage. The Catholic Church accepted Christ as the first pope with this Bible passage. Believers in the Messiah, led by St. Barnabas, gathered there for a year after the construction of the church, and were called Christians (Acts of the Apostles 12:26).

Although faith in the Messiah appeared in the Middle East, in Jerusalem, it is curious that some of the apostles were able to make it to Anatolia and Antakya in such a short amount of time after Christ's resurrection. The answer to this lies in the Pentecost day in the New Testament in the book Acts of the Apostles. Jewish people living outside of Israel used to gather to pray in their own languages a few times during the year. During one of these times they could hear and understand the happy news in their own languages by a miracle of God. What was this miracle? Some of the Jewish people accepted Christ as their salvation, taking Him as the Messiah mentioned in the Old Testament. The ideas and principles pointed out by Jesus Christ were not unfamiliar to them and, moreover, Jesus Christ was not claiming to have brought a new faith. He was commenting on the practices of Moses' Judaism. At the beginning, Christianity was more like a Jewish sect.

St. Paul:

Paul, who was known as Saul before becoming one of the apostles, was also present at these meetings as a committed Jew. At the beginning, as a committed Pharisee, Paul was against believers of this new faith. He was born in 10 B.C. in Tarsus, Anatolia. His real name was Saul. Actually, his name is mentioned as Saul in the book Acts of the Apostles. Like many Jews in the region, as a Roman citizen he was using a Roman name that was given to him by his family and learned crafts and became a tent-maker. He received religious education in Jerusalem. In Rome, political integration was critical. Under the umbrella of the Roman belief system every ethnicity had to be respectful to others even if they didn't get along. Only one community was having a hard time acting accordingly: Jews. They were quite stubborn to protect their traditions and beliefs. Romans were not able to put Greek mythology in the Jewish belief system. Fundamentalist believers were getting stricter about the new faith as they grew stronger in the empire. Paul was one such Jew and he contributed to the persecution of the first Christian martyr, Stephen. He vandalized the church and despised the believers of the new faith. As related in the book Acts of the Apostles, while Saul was traveling to Damascus with a letter from the Jewish authorities suddenly a strong light appeared in the sky, he fell off his horse, and a voice from heaven said to him: *"Saul, why do you persecute me?.." and* Saul asked. *"Who are you, Lord?.."* Woice replied: *"I am Jesus, whom you are persecuting.."* (Acts of the Apostles 9:5).

This was a turning point in Saul's life. As an apostle, he turned into the greatest defender of the Christian faith. He had long journeys to spread Christianity, led communities, and wrote letters to non-believers. He did most of this work in Anatolia. Cappadocia used to be one of the Roman states and, like the other states, lived under certain regulations. People were tired of heavy taxes and economical instability. In a way, Christianity was another way of showing displeasure to the Romans. It was born in Palestine but it got bigger and stronger in Anatolia. Anatolia had an important place in Paul's life as he, himself, repeated many times in his letters.

St.Basil (Great Basileos):

The Great Basileos was born on 329 and died on 379 in Caesarea(todays Kayseri). He was a scholar that wrote many books and texts on religion. Also he has created a structure of the Eastern Church ideas,principles and community. After his death he was granted the Sainthood. There is a small Chapel at Göreme open air museum on his memory. The Christians of Cappadocia has kept the holy memory df their Saint for centuries.

Gregory of Nyssa:

He was born in Caesarea in 335. He was a famous law and phylosophy man also a rulling figure of the church.His knowledge on religion comes from his brother Basileos and Gregory of Nazianzos. When he was the bishop of Nyssa on 371 he fought the opposite ideas like Arius. He died on 394 and his death was accepted 9th March feast.

Gregory of Nazianzos:

He is one of the 3 saints of Cappadocia who lived in the 4th century He was born on 330 in Nazianzos(Nenezi) and died on 371 at Arianzos. He also fought the Arius Ideas like his brother Gregorius of Nyssa and his friend Great Basil. The eastern churches feast is celebrated on 25 and 30 January.

The story of St.Gregory:

There are a lot of churches called the Serpent Church in göreme, Ihlara and Soğanlı walleys because of the themes of snakes (dragon) scened on churches walls. The image of the snake sometimes between two warriors with spears on their hands on horseback. One warior is St. Gregory, the other is St. Theodor.

The legend states that there was a huge dragon living near the waterfront of Hallays, which this beast was always feeding on the live stock of the peasats. One day when the dragon was about to attack a beautiful girl down at the waterfront, Gregorius was passing by which he killed the dragon with his spear and saved the girl.

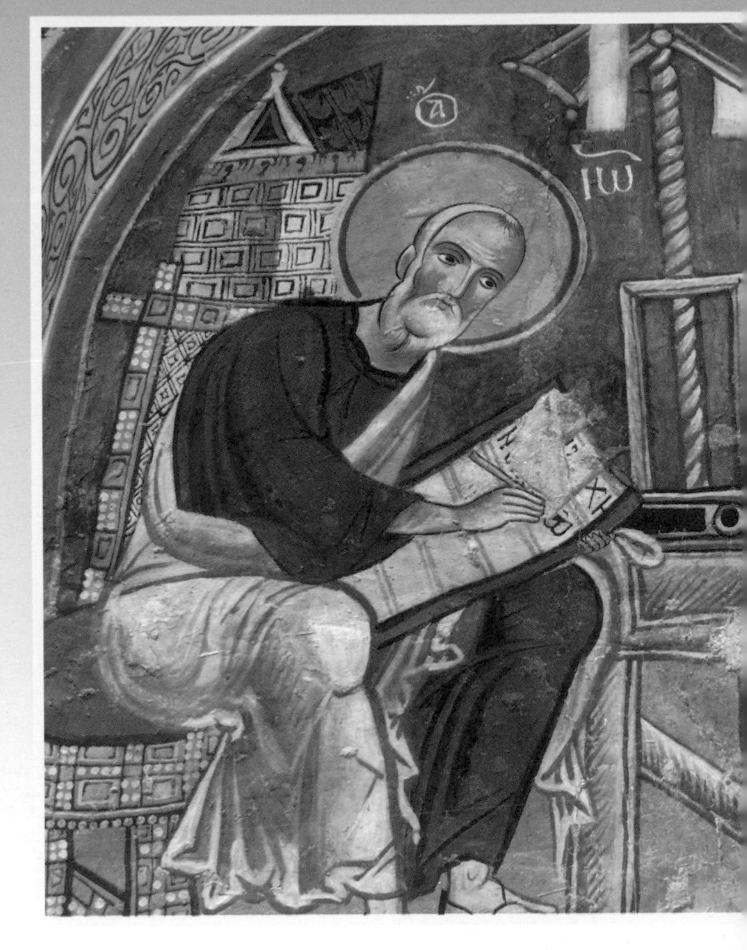

The Dark Church.Crucifixion (left) und St.Paulus (top).

Saint Barbara:

She was born a daughter of a non-believer called Dios Corios . She is a Saint lived in Nicomedia (İzmit), in the 2nd. c.B.C. When she started believing Christianity, she goes to her father to announce her belief, her outraged father took her to Praefectus (high commander of Rome) this person orders her to be killed. Her father wolunteers for this job and cuts his own daughter like a lamb, but the Holy Father sends a lightning and bunrs the father. Upon this incedent Barbara was granted Sainthood and a Chapelle has been built in her name just opposite Yılanlı Kilise (Serpent Church) at Monastery Valley(Open air museum) of Göreme.

The Monastery Valley of Göreme (Open air museum) (top)

The Plan of Open air Museum (right)
1) Nun's Monastery 2) St.Basil Chapel 3-9-10-16) Dining Halls 4) Elmalı Church 5) St.Barbara Church 6) Yılanlı Church 7) St.Onophrius Church 8) Catacomb 11) St.Katherine Chapel 12) Dark Church 13) Çarıklı(Sandal)Church 14-15) Chapel

After 17 km from Nevsehir, you reach a 32 km² volcanic valley ancient name of which is Korama with fairy chimneys.

In 1705 the French explorer **Paul Lucas** who was sent by Louis 14th. to middle-east, especially to Ottoman land, was shocked when he arrived in Ürgüp on the way to Kayseri. He was enchanted by the fairy chimneys and people living in them, churches, pigeon houses, and beautiful valleys of Cappadocia region.

Fairy chimneys in Göreme Valley (engraving of Paul Lucas-1741).

Rock Churches of Cappadocia:
(Open Air Museum of Göreme)

When he was back in France, he published his traveling notes in 1712. He states that he first thought that the fairy chimneys were tombs of a lost civilization but when he looked into them he realized that they were dwellings carved into the rock. He calls the structures that he saw pyramids, and he actually exaggerates when he is defining the place. The travel book creates a lot of debates in public, but also it starts interest about the area. Lucas returns back to the region in 1714 to reexamine the area. Neraly 130 years later, an architect called Charles Texier visited the area. He wrote a detailed report of his inspections between 1833-37 including plans and pictures under the name **Researches on Asia Minor**. Texier published the part about Göreme Valley in Cappadocia in the **Le Monde Illustrated** magazine telling about how dazed he was to see the area. Later, W.F. Ainsworth (1842), geologist W.J. Hamilton (1837) and Prussian Marshall Moltke (1838 Nevsehir-Urgup) also visited the region. In 1864, British architect R.P. Pullan (Urgup), in the beginning of the 20th century Ger-

Yusuf Koç Church, Göreme: Portraits of Saints.

man H. Rott (Aksaray-Selime), and French R.P.Guillaume De Jerphanion (1907-1912/Göreme) followed the first foreign visitors of the region. Jerphanion made an extensive research of the churches, monasteries, and frescos and publish a report called **Rock Churches of Cappadocia**. As a result, the interest in visiting the area grew bigger. Actually, the whole area was started to be called Göreme as it was the main focus of many reports. The frescos that R.P.Guillaume De Jerphanion found were from 9th and 11th centuries. There was only a chapel from 7th century. Göreme that was one of the significant centers in early Byzantine times was actually structured in Iconoclast era. When Empress Theodora stopped the ban on Icons, monastery life was resumed under Byzantine influence. Tokali and Kiliclar churches are important examples from the churches built during that time. When the Arabian attacks ceased during the reign of Nicephoros Phocas in 956, the monastery life came out of the underground cities. With 11th century, a total aristocratic period began in church art. The descriptions of the paintings in this period are very different from the early Byzantine era. The paintings and compositions were done by accomplished artists working for the emperor. In terms of architecture, columns were used as well as a center dome instead of a cruciform vault. Çarıklı Church, Elmalı

Benedictions of Saints (top)
The Annunciation (Dark Church) (right).

Church and Karanlık Church are good illustration of the architectural tradition of this era. After 11th century, frescos started to be made more crudely. The use of stone blocks brought the more common use of wooden Icons.

Göreme Valley and the rock churches are open to public visit as an **Open Air Museum** today. It is believed that there are hundreds of other churches in the area other than the already discovered well-known ones. Until these are also found, the restoration of the ones that we already know is going to go on to secure a treasure that has been passed on for many generations from the damage of nature and humans. Let's learn about the most popular churches and rock structures of the Göreme Valley.

Altar of the Dark Church:
Virgin Mary, Jesus and St.John the Baptist (left).
Crucifixion (top) and The Nativity (right).

The Dark Church

It is a two floor church that was built in 11th century with a lot of care. Cradle vaulted rectangular narthex of the church is reached via a curved ladder. As the front of the rock that the church was carved into collapsed, most of the ceiling and some parts of the main- room wall is in open air. It actually was designed as a monastery with the upper floor the ceiling of which is different as it was designed to accommodate monks.

The entry to the main church from the corridor is through an arched, bordered door that is reached

Η ΜΕΤΑ
ΜΟΡΦΟϹΙϹ
ΙϹ
ΧϹ
ΠΕΤΡΟϹ

Transfiguration (left).
The dome of the Dark church: Jesus the Pantocrator(top)
Ressurection (right).

with a couple of stairs. The church was built under a center dome. The reason of being named as Karanlık (Dark) Church is that it takes a very small amount of light from a small window in the narthex part. For this reason, the colors in the frescos painted on the wall are very lively. They are similar to the ones in Çarıklı and Elmalı Church.

Scenes: Ascension, Benedictions of Saints, Hospitality of Abraham, Ascension, Betrayal of Judas, Womens from Galile, Mary, Klaofas, Maria Magdalena, Moses' wife, Judgement of Pontus Pilate, the last supper, Crucifixion, Transfiguration, The Nativity, Joseph and Mary, Adoration of Maggi's, journey to Bethlehem, Ordeal, Anastasis, Passion and Ressurection.

IC XC

The Nativity, New Tokalı (left).
New Tokalı, an interior view of Narthex (top).
Mary and little Jesus (right).

The Tokalı Church

It is the biggest known ancient rock church of the region. The structure and the paintings have been kept well. It consist two churches that were built in two different times. The entrance is called **Old Tokalı**. The life of Christ is divided into panels and depicted in a way that looks like a comic strip in the main room. Green, brown, and red are dominant colors. The sharp movements of the lines that create the design of the embellishments make it look very dynamic. It is **Syrian and Cappadocian** in style and was built in the beginning of the 10th century. The painter had chance to tell different sto-

Crucifixion (top). The Annunciation (below), The presentation of Mary to Temple (top right) and Benedictions of the Saints(below right).

ries as the place is relatively more divided by columns and naves. The arch over the columns with the small frieze and the pediment at the very top remind us of a theater stage. It is designed in a Greco-Roman style.

Scenes: Annunciation, Baptism, journey to Bethlehem, Nativity, The escape of Mary with John, At Cana, Jeremiah and Ezekiel, The Judgement of Pilate, Entrance to Jerusalem, Transfiguration, Presentation of Virgin Mary to Temple, Flight to Egypt, Adoration of Maggi's, Martyr of Zechariah, miracles in Cana, charging the disciples, recovery of the blind man, resurrection of Lazarus, Crucifixion, Descent from the cross, The Entombment, Ascen-

Jesus, Virgin Mary and St.John the Baptist (left).
Jesus the Pantocrator (top). The Betrayal of Judas(detail)(right).

The Çarıklı Church

It has two floors, and was built in 11th century. It is not know how the entry of the church was constructed at the time. The church that is reached after iron stairs is cross-vaulted and domed.

It is thought that the church is named as **Çarıklı (Sandal) Church** because of the carvings opposite to the entrance that are shaped as footprints. Downstairs, there are three rooms one of which being the dining room. The paintings are not in good shape.

Scenes: Christ sitting on a throne with Mary on the left and Saint John the Baptist on the right, Nativity, hospitality of Prophet Abraham, Resurrection of Lazarus, Crucifixion, and three angels waiting by Christ's grave.

Crucifixion(left)
Jesus, Virgin Mary and St.John the Baptist (top).
Jesus the Pantokrator (right).

Elmalı Church

The name **Elmalı**(with Apple) comes from the apple trees around it. Since the main room is collapsed, entrance can be made through a tunnel. It has four columns, a closed Greek cross plan and three abscissas. The scenes painted on the walls are in harmony with the structure of the building. The high window on the east wall provides very good lighting.

Scenes: Baptism of Christ(water ordeal) in the river by Saint John, Resurrection, Crucifixion, Angels by Christ's grave, Christ etnthorned by a holy scene(Middle Dome), Portraits of the Bible writers, Alias, Daniel, Jonas and Moses, Christ, Virgin Mary and Saint John the Baptist.

The Altar of St.Catherine Chapel (top). Detail from the barrel vault of Yılanlı Chunch (top right). St.Barbara Church and Ikonoklastic symbols (below right).

TheYılanlı Church and St.Catherine Chapel

The Yılanlı(Serpent) Church ın The main place has a longitudinal rectangular plan, is cradle vaulted and the additional place in the south has a flat ceiling. The church is dated to the 11th century. There is a door with two columns and an arch behind the oriel. It does not have a typical altar. Across the entrance on the absyde, in the ceiling St Basil, St Thomas, St. Onophrius are depicted as well as St George and St Theodore.

St.Catherine Chapel is between the Karanlık (Dark) Church and Çarıklı (Sandal) Church. Both narthex and naos are free cross planned and central domed; the cross arms are cradle vaulted and the abscissa is with templons. There are nine graves on the narthex floor and two niche graves on the walls.

The church was built by a woman named Anna in 11th century. There are figures only in naos part of the chapel. Pandantives are covered with relief like geometric ornaments.

Scenes: Deesis in temploned absis, below this church fathers in medallions, (St.Gregory, St.Basil, St.John the Baptist), on southern wall of northern cross arm St.George on horseback, across it St. Theodore, St Catherine and other saint pictures.

St.Barbara Church

It has one main floor with one main, two supplementary abscissas. The door to the church is a crown door with a little patio. It is mostly destroyed. It has two columns with a cradle vaulted center that is domed. It is from the second part of the 11th century. The symbols are directly drawn on rock with red paint. It is highly probable that the paintings and the embellishments are from different periods. There are some symbols on the walls, although they seem to be from the Iconoclast period. On altar Christ the Pantocrator, St. George fighting with a dragon on horseback, St Theodore and St. Barbara, Flight to Egypt scenes can be seen. It seems like a temple that mainly used for funerals.

Views from Nun's Monastery ad its rock massive.
And a Hermitage room with frescoes inside the rock complex (left).

Nun's Monastery

The rock massive consisting of 6 floors located at the left of the Goreme open-air museum entrance is known as **Nun's Monastery**.

This monastery has a dining hall, a kitchen, and a few rooms are on the first and second floors. Its church on the 3rd floor (that is reached through a tunnel) has a cross dome. Millstone like round **Bolt stones** are used for closing the tunnels in case of a danger as in the case for the underground cities like Derinkuyu.

Exterior of the Church(left). and the Interior of the church with "Ascension" scene in dome (top).

El Nazar Church

This church was carved into a tent-formed rock in a **T** plan. That's why it might look like a cross shaped church. It can be dated to 10th century.

It is cruciform with three apses, the main apse opening up in the center where the cradle vaulted arms of the cruciform meet. It has two floors. The entry was probably downstairs that opened up to the second floor with a flight of stairs. As one of the sides was collapsed, it was covered after renovation to protect the paintings from the effect of natural forces. The paintings are in perfect harmony with the structure of the church. They are different characters from the other churches of Göreme, seems to be a special church.

Scenes are : Christ enthroned a holy scene, the Benediction of the Saints, portrait of the Saints framed, and Christ surrounded by saints and angels in a medallion(Ascension) and The Nativity.

The old Çavuşin. Abondoned rock dwellings and settlements.

Çavuşin and the Nicephoros Phocas II. Church

Cavuşin is 2.5km away from Goreme-Avanos road. Basically houses surround a mountain like massive rock. It is all messed up as a result of the erosion of the rocks over time and earthquakes. There are relatively new stone buildings in front of old stone blocks. You can see domed structures that get higher towards the top of the rock as well as praying buildings, monks caves and shelters among the houses. They look like an ant colony looking from above. Saint Baptist Monastery, which is one of the oldest buildings in Cappadocia, is hidden among the rocks here. It is an enormous basilica carved in the top part of the rock.

Nicephoros Phocas Church (Çavuşin Church) is beside Göreme Avanos road, 2.5 km far from Göreme. It has single nave, cradle vault, 3 abscis-

Nikophoros Phokas Church and its rock-massive (top).
The abondoned entrance of the church (right)

sas and its narthex has been destroyed. The Church that has been constructed in the name of Emperor Nicephoros Phocas is dated to the year 964 - 965. The themes used in the church are taken from the Bible and the life of Christ as in other churches. And inside the entrance of the main hall, portraits of Nicephoros Phocas and his family can be seen.

PAŞABAĞ

Typical fairy chimneys of Paşabağ (top and left) Back page: Different views from the region.

When you are driving on the way to Avanos from Goreme, having driven through Cavuşin, you can see fairy chimney through the grapevines and fruit trees that look like giant monks that are running up the hill. Some of them have more than one head with interesting body shapes. Some of them has actually more than one body. A fairy chimney with three heads for instance is known as **Hermitage of St. Simon** . In 5th century, Saint Simon came to the region to live on a fairy chimney to get rid of the people of Jerusalem who started to disturb him after the rumors that he created miracles. Then, he moved into the fairy chimney with three heads that is higher than the first one. This fairy chimney is dated to the 10th century and it houses two rooms including the praying room that is reached by a steep flight of stairs. The town has attracted many monks who were looking for some solitary place. We cannot tell anything about the number of monks who sheltered in the fairy chimneys that seemed like nothing but a massive rock. But another name for the town is the **Monks Valley** which means the valley of the monks.

Zelve. An important region of the Monastic life in times. Back page: Different views from Zelve.

ZELVE

Zelve is one of the oldest and most famous parts of the rocky Cappadocia region. The monasteries and churches from the times when the Christianity was a new developing faith are good examples of the inhabitances of the time. There are two big churches on the sides of the valley. There is a cross with fishes on its arms that is truly unique as something similar has never been found in any other place in the region. There are other chapels and churches on the hills open to public. There are many paintings of crosses that are good examples of the **Iconoclastic symbolism** of the time. The fact that there are not a lot of religious depictions might tell us that people were against Icons even before Iconoclast movement. Later, Muslims started to move into the region, which can be understood, by the mosques in the area. Zelve is having hard days today as it might collapse.

Derbent and its interesting rock formations.

DERBENT

The valley where you can take camel tours is also called the pink valley. It is possible to see interesting rock formations from the road that goes through the valley. Unfortunately, in 2004 some fairy chimneys was destroyed by the power of the nature that created it. On the way, having passed the camel, it is possible to see dolphins and even a penguin and a camel. On your right is Mother Mary with surrounded by a couple of human statues. Although, there are not any churches nearby, the weird rocks formations are quite appealing to the imagination of the people who likes to walk around.

The Pancarlı Valley in Ürgüp and famous fairy chimneys of Ürgüp (left and top). Back page: The "Hallaç" Monastery and the "Pancarlı" Church.

ÜRGÜP

Ürgüp is a lovely town situated 23km from Nevsehir. The town is in the middle of the Cappadocia area near Kızılırmak(Hallys), between Tekke and Topuz mountains in the east, Avla and Germil mountains in the south. The name Ürgüp comes from Hittite word **Ur-Kup** (Many Castles). Saint Paul visited once during his well-known journeys in Anatolia. The whole area became famous in the world thanks to **Paul Lucas** who came to Urgup in 18th century. When he was back in France, he described Urgup as **The fantastic cemetery of a destroyed civilization** in his traveling notes. R.P. Guillaume and Jerphanion who later visited the region Examined the churches carved into rock from a closer perspective and introduced the area to the world again. Urgup is also interesting in the sense that it has houses that are typically from Cappadocia region built using stone blocks or carved into the rock. These are pretty little houses that were carved into the rock and were supported by stone blocks that were made out of the same rock.

Examples of Seljuk and Ottoman art can be seen in Ürgüp. The tomb of Altıkapı, Nukreddin Tomb, Tahir Ağa Library, the Underground Gateway and the Archeology and Ethnography museums are among the well-known and popular places to visit.

Beautiful houses of Mustafapaşa (Sinassos) (top)
The entrance of St.Vasilius Church (right)

Mustafapaşa

It is 5km south of Urgup. The ancient name of the town **Sinassos** (**Sinuwa-Assos** in Luwi language) means the **city**/town with/**abounding in fish**. The name might be coming from the fact that the town was founded near a small stream called Damsa. In the town center and in Kemerlidere, there are rock houses. The main attraction in town is the stone houses with ornamented walls that are supreme examples of the art from 19th century, an art that was passed from generation to generation in those times. The major historical places in the town are: Holy Apostles Church, Saint Vassili Church, Saint Basil Church, and Tavsanli Church.

The Rock-castle of Ortahisar (left) and Typical stone houses of the region (top).

ORTAHİSAR

Ortahisar is a small town in Ürgüp. It is on the motorway from Kayseri to Nevşehir just 1 km from Ürgüp. The town was one of the important mountain passes in the past. It is a significant town with the ancient monasteries and churches and with its famous castle that was carved into the rock. People who were executed in the developing stages of Christianity took shelter in this castle. Even during the time when Seljuks were controlling the area, Christian and Muslim people running away from the Mongolian attacks moved into this castle. Towards north in the midst of the grapevines there is a chapel belonging to Nicetas paintings of which have survived over the time. The main historical monuments in Ortahisar are Canbazli church that was another Byzantine village church, Saint Paul and Saint Peter churches in Meskender Dere, a church from 11th century in Kepez, Hallac Monastery, and churches in Balkan Deresi. Ibrahim Pasha (Babayan) and Uzengidere.

Typical Fairy chimneys and rock dwellings of Uçhisar (left). The rock-castle of Uçhisar and environs (top).

UÇHİSAR

Uçhisar is a small town on the Nevsehir-Ürgüp motorway. It is on the highest part of the valley that it was founded in. Like Ortahisar, this town also gets the name from its castle. The castle that was built on a massive rock and is believed to have been built by Hittites is an indication of the strategic importance of the town, which was on the Silk Road once. The fairy chimney colonies with their unique grey color on the lower skirts of the castle are like big apartment buildings housing many people even today. If you own or have rented a fairy chimney to live, it means that you have a mansion that is the same temperature all through the year and clean from any bugs. If you need some extra space, you always have the chance to carve the rock to create another room. The amazing view of the other fairy chimneys overlooking the breathtaking valley comes for free, and of course delicious wine of the region. When you are on the top of the castle, you can see the whole valley till Göreme. The land under your feet look wild and endless, which is unique with the white, yellow and pink rock formations. The typical dovecuts of the region are extension of an old tradition. Beside making rugs and crafting onyx stone, the people of the region also make jewelry out of dark blue apatite stone.

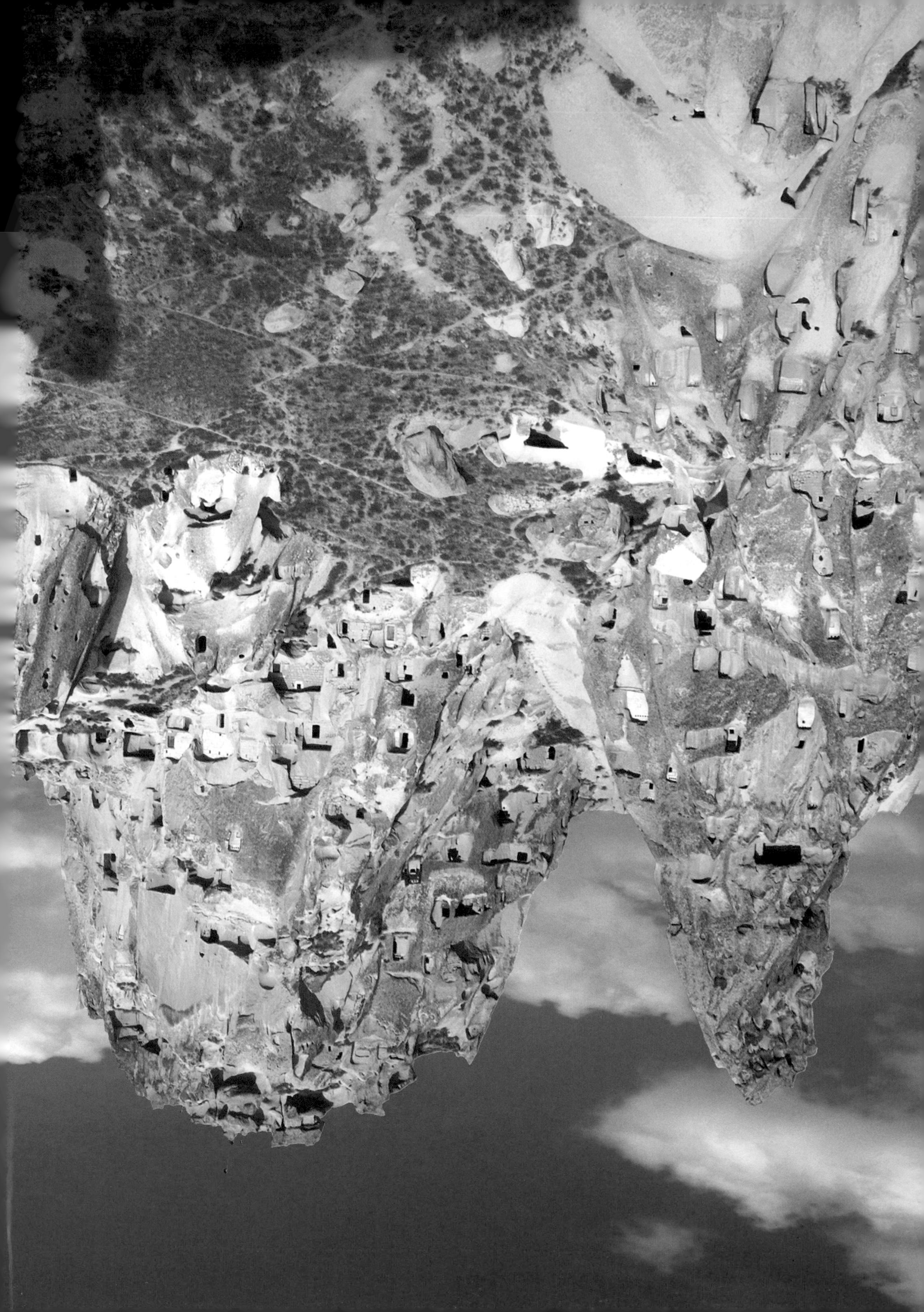

IHLARA CANYON

A view from IhlaraCanyon and Melendiz river.

*I*n the northeast of Hasan Mountain, **Peristrema** or **Belisırama** in Turkish language Canyon extends for 14km by the banks of the Melendiz River born in Melendiz Mountains between **Selime** and **Yaprakhisar**. Peristremma means **curvy** in Hellenic languagc. Today, it is called Ihlara Canyon. Ihlara village is on the south side of the canyon. The canyon shaped after greenish Trakyt rocks 100-200m high were broken is captivating with the wild natural beauty and monastery ambiance craving for solitude. The fairy chimneys and castle of Selime (Salomon) embellishes one side of the valley.

In 1958, **Nicole and Michelle Thierry** got a better understanding of the churches that were also examined by H. Rott, Ramsay, and Bell at the beginning of the 20th century. The big rock pieces that fell off the canyon cover the steep, curvy paths. It was very difficult to spot the churches among all that rock. When Thierry couple examined what they were able to find, they actually drew different conclusions from what R.P Guillaume de Jer-

Ağaçaltı Church's Dome. "Ascention".

phanion had in his book **Cappadocia Rock Churches**. In their book that they wrote between the years of 1958-1963, they categorized the churches into two in terms of the symbols and depictions. The ones around **Ihlara** were very different from those built in Cappadocia or Byzantium style. They were more related to Egyptian, Roman even Sasani and early Christian art. In all the pictures, the bible stories were described in a symbolic way. The churches in this group include: Egritaş,Yılanlı, Kokar, Purenliseki(4th century) and Ağaçaltı (5th century) Churches. The ones in the middle of the Canyon and around **Belisirama** have more Byzantine characteristic like: Bahaeddin Samanlığı, Direkli, Sumbullu, and Kirkdamalti (13th century) Churches.

The Arabic attacks that started in 7th century was not able to penetrate in monastery life as a result of the geographical structure of the region, and after the control was taken over was Byzantium in the middle of the 10th century increased the number of churches. Ala, Karagedik(11th century) Churches were built in this period. Aksaray was an important religious centre even in the early years of

Yılanlı Church, The Martyrs of Sebast top).
Angel Michael (right).

Christianity. St.**Basil the Great** and **Gregory from Nazianz** were born in this region and they created the rules of a monastery life that is different from Syrian-Egyptian way here. As a result, Greek-Slavic monastery system was born. In Egypt and Syrian monasteries, the monks would totally isolate themselves from the pleasures of the world by dedicating themselves only God. St.Gregory and St.Basil-claimed that it was appropriate for the monks to work and be helpful and useful to the world. This system spread in Slav and Greek world formed the bases of post-Byzantium Christian faith.

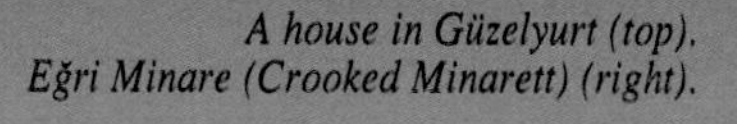

A house in Güzelyurt (top).
Eğri Minare (Crooked Minarett) (right).

AKSARAY

Aksaray name of which comes from **Archelaos**, the last king of the Cappadocia, is 60 miles northeast of Konya. The monuments, castles and their legends tell us that the region that Aksaray is in was under the control of the Hittites for a very long time. The Hellene name of the city was **Garsaura** that comes from the Hittite word **Kursaura** that meant the holy river in Hittite language. It was an important city during both Seljuks and Romans as it was in a position to control the ways that connect Kayseri to Capadocia and Ankara to Taurus Mountains. The city was under Karamanoğlu rule for a while. Eventually, Ottomans took control of the city.

The Mosque-church (St. Gregory Church).

Güzelyurt and the Monastery Valley

Güzelyurt is situated 15km from Ihlara valley. It is 40km southeast of Aksaray. Guzelyurt, Gelveri with it ancient name, come from **Karballa** in **Luwi** language, means **small hill**/zenith of a small hill. There are underground dwellings built by Hittites in the town center and on **Cevizli Street**. After that Karballa was homeland to Assyrian trade colonies, Meds, Persians, Cappadocian Kingdom, Romans, Byzantines, Seljuks, and Ottomans. When the Christianity grew stronger in the area, father and son Gregory turned the town into an important center. Gelveri was a village in the borders of Naziansos (Nenenzi). The doctrines of Gregory the theologian created a new branch of Christianity here. There is a church named **Mosque-Church** in Guzelyurt that has the holy reminds of Gregory. Guzelyurt is a small model of Cappadocia containing everything typical to the region with underground cities, churches and fairy chimneys. The major rock churches of the town include **Yuksek Kilise**(High Church) and **Kızıl Kilise**(Red Church-at Sivrihisar).

Monastery Valley is more like an extension to the Ihlara valley. In the valley tha is 4.5km, there is a spring which has been there for a long time. On the hill next to the valley is the underground city of "Ishalka" that is said to have housed 30,000 people. It is believed that the monastery life first started here in 3-4th centuries BC.

Since prehistoric times, people have lived in caves that they chiseled out of stone. During the ice ages, the climate was very harsh and people used natural cavities in the rock to survive. People started to chisel soft tufa rocks to build galleries, shelters, prayer rooms, and tombs that resembled the habitat of an ant colony. The people of Cappadocia preferred to be living on the sides of mountains however, in case of danger or need; they carved more dwellings into the rock. This lifestyle went on for centuries and, at the beginning of the time of Christianity, people living in underground cities, isolated themselves from the rest of the world used these places.

The Underground city of Derinkuyu. The secrets of Anatolian people throughout the history.

The Underground Cities of Cappadocia

The Cappadocia region was occupied by different cultures during its history. People who normally dwell in houses would move into these underground caves with their domestic animals for security purposes. These dwellings, which could only be reached by hidden entrances, were used at different times and were modified to meet the varied needs of its occupants. The underground cities were also connected to the above-ground houses in the area. The cities had hundreds of rooms that were connected with long, narrow tunnels and corridors. At the ends of the tunnels, there were millstone like cylindrical bolt stones used to seal the tunnels. The bolt stones were 200-300kg, 30-50cm thick, and 1-1.5 meters in diameter. These stones were carved in the tunnels out of massive rocks, and they were put over the entry from a room behind the entryway. Attackers could be seen through holes in the middles of the stones. They were even killed using lances. All of the underground cities and inhabitances differed as a result of the geographical conditions and the purposes of the buildings. However, they all shared common characteristics. They all had large stables where all the animals were kept together, which was on the first floor or near the entry. They all had long carved chimneys were used for air conditioning and communication between dwellings. They all had dining rooms, bedrooms, kitchens with stone stoves, chapels and wineries. There were cavities chiseled into the walls to put oil lamps and earthenware pots of food and to hang things. There were also, toilets and septic wells. We see examples of all these in Güzelyurt (Gelveri) and Tatlarin. There were even wells that had fake connections above-ground to prevent the enemy from poisoning the water, as well as rooms where the dead were temporarily stored before the actual burial.

Historian **Strabon**(84 BC- 17AD), indicated in his famous book **Geography** that, although the area from Lycaonia to Caeserea including Malegob is not even irrigated, the wells there are the deepest in the world. Another writer from ancient times, **Xenophon** (430-355 BC), talks about the underground cities as: "...*The houses in the villages were constructed under the ground. The entrances to the houses were very narrow, more like the mouth of a well. However, the rooms were pretty wide. The animals were also kept in the same rooms chiseled underground, and there were special tunnels for them to get in and out. You would not know or see the entrances to these tunnels. But humans were using ladders to get into animals' rooms. There were sheep, goats, poultry, cattle, and their offspring...*" and adds: "... *people of these villages produced beer with barley and they would use pipes to drink when they got thirsty and they would add some more water when they were done drinking. The grapes in this area are very good to make wine–they made wine in these underground rooms- and we were given a lot wine in sheepskin bags when we left...*"

There are a total of 200 dwellings that are known in the area. We can guess the total number of people living in these inhabitances by comparing them to the same number of villages in terms of population. There used to be linseed oil lamps to illuminate

An Interior view from the Underground city of Kaymaklı. Passways to different places (top).

these dark rooms and caves. Boiling hot linseed oil was also used to surprise the enemy when it was poured down onto anyone trying to pass through the narrow corridors. Probably because of the insulating character of the tufa rock the average temperature is 14-16 Celsius degrees in all seasons, Linseed oil lamps were also used for heating. Although we know that people of the region used **Obsidien**, which was ample in the Neolithic period, to chisel the rocks, the artifacts found tell us that starting from 3,000 B.C. metal was used more commonly in the area. Some of the dwellings were also occupied by Hittites for different purposes. There were Hittite stone legends found in and around the dwellings. From the time of the Hittites onward, metal was

The underground city of Derinkuyu. The Basilica (top),
A tunnel from the underground city of Acıgöl (right).

used to shape the rocks, as can be understood from the way the rocks were shaped – probably by handy craftsmen who were good at using the metal tools that they had. Today, the craft of shaping rocks is passed from generation to generation.

Unfortunately, no tools or pieces of furniture have been found in underground cities so far. This might show us that these dwellings were used temporarily and when the need to use them ceased, with the end of the oppression on Christian communities, they were evacuated according to plan and not fled from. All of these comments are only valuable with a close examination of the area. New discoveries are illuminating the unknown aspects of the life in underground.

E
B
B
B
B
B
© 2007 Melih ÖNDÜN

General Construction of an Underground City
Entrance
Passageway
Winery
Living room
Church
Grave
Storage
Stairs
Bolt Stone
Chimney-Well
Oven
Bedroom
Toilet-Bain
Exit
Stable
Closed Area

The underground city of Derinkuyu. A millstone (left), and the Church (top).

Derinkuyu and Kaymaklı

Derinkuyu and Kaymaklı are both found in a wide, low basin on the Nevşehir-Niğde motorway where the Melendiz mountain range gets lower, beginning with Hasan Mountain. There are no springs, but there are many wells and underground rivers that have been known about since ancient times. Derinkuyu, old names of which are Malahopea or Melegop, is 25km from Nevşehir. The underground dwelling that was opened to public in 1965 is 40m deep according to the chimney-like air-conditioning tunnel. However, if the well that has no connection with the ground is included, the total depth is 85m. There are 52 vertical air tunnels in Derinkuyu. The bottom parts of these chimney-like tunnels are water wells. Until 1962, the water needed by the people living in the town of Derinkuyu was gotten from these wells by pulleys. It is believed that nearly 30 dwellings, that are connected to each other via tunnels, accommodated 10,000 people at the time. Derinkuyu, with its 8 floors and total size of 2.5km2 is estimated to be the biggest underground city in the world. The place holds all of the characteristics of an underground city. Although there are 8 floors open today, the actual size of the city is unknown.

1st Floor: There is a stable, a passageway, a winery, living rooms, a church and a missionary school. 2nd Floor: There is a kitchen and a winery, and the

The underground city of Kaymaklı (top and right).
The underground city of Özkonak. A typical door system (left).

living rooms. 3rd Floor: There is storage rooms for food, the chimney-like air shafts.

4th Floor: It is on the way to the exit and it has living rooms with provision depots. The gallery that starts on the third floor directly goes up to the 5th floor. The bolt stone with a hole is used to block the entryway to the gallery. 5th and 6th Floors: There is an air shaft that is connected to the ground on this floor, rooms, two bolt stones. 7th Floor: There is a church with a crucifix plan with three columns, a water well that has no connection to the outside of the city, a tomb room and an auditorium with three columns opposite to the church. 8th Floor: It only has one little room and an air shaft.

Underground city of Kaymaklı is 15-25m deep. In Kaymaklı village was called as **Enegüp**, the people built their houses around approximately 100

tunnels. The city plan and construction of Kaymaklı is different from Derinkuyu. The corridors are narrow and leaning, and the ceiling is low. The rooms are gathered around the vertical air-conditioning tunnels. Four floors have been unearthed. 1st Floor: There is a stable. The small corridor with a bolt stone and daily living rooms. 2nd Floor: There is a church and living rooms and platforms to be used as seats on both sides.

3rd Floor: The most important locations of the underground city are on this floor. When you are on way down, you can see the storage rooms. 4th Floor: There is a winery and storage area. There are kitchens on this wing of the floor. Although all of the sections of the underground city have not been cleared yet, it is certain that it is one of the biggest underground dwellings in the area. When we consider the number of storage rooms in such a small area, it can be concluded that there were a lot of people living in this inhabitance.

Özkonak

The underground city is situated in Özkonak Town that is 14 km away from Avanos, on the northern slopes of İdiş Mountain. The underground city has not been completely cleaned yet, but the galleries spread to cleaned large areas are connected to each other through tunnels. Unlike the underground cities in Kaymakli and Derinkuyu, there are very narrow (5 cm) and long holes between the different levels of the city that used to provide communication between the different levels of the city.

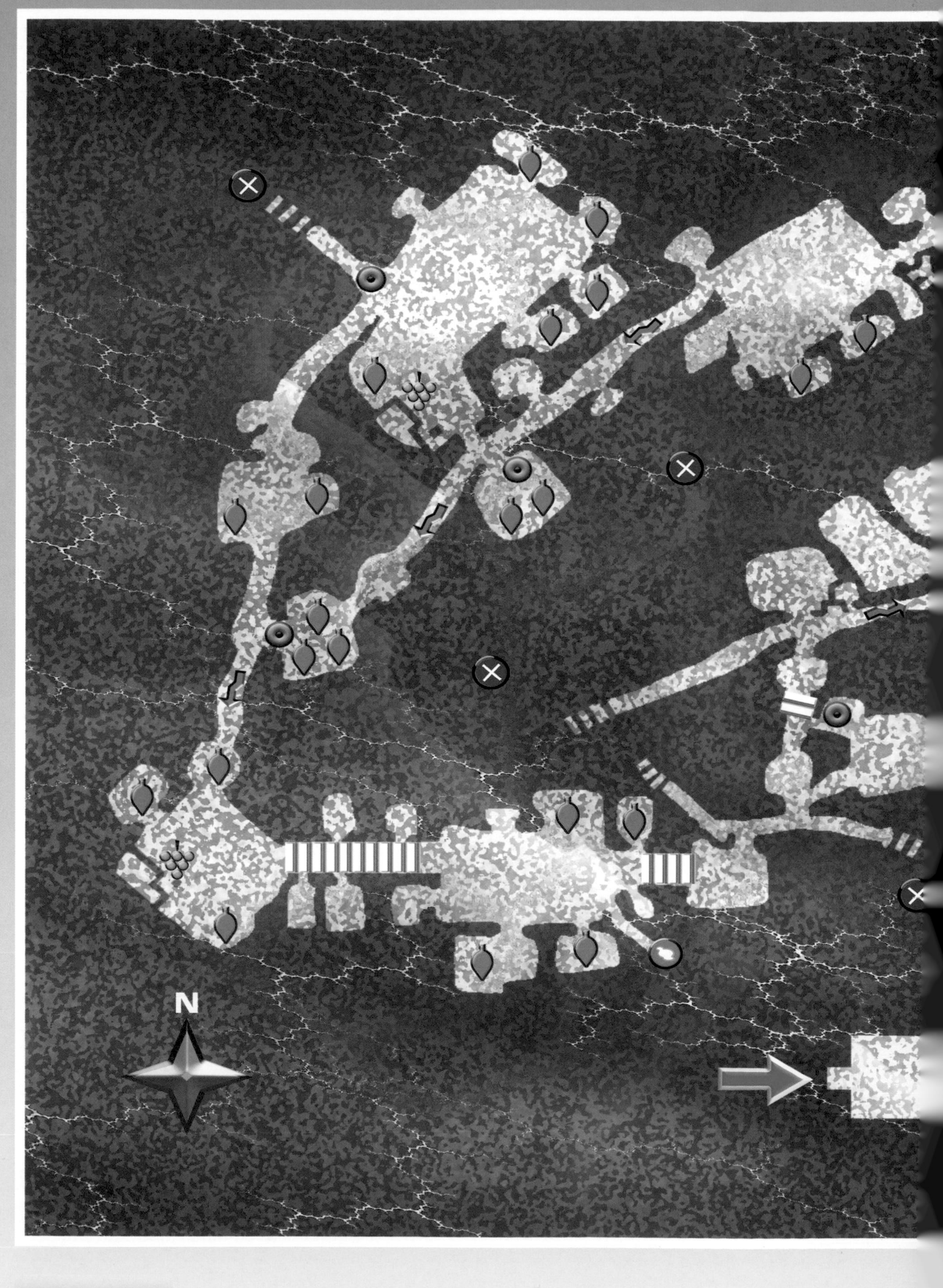
N

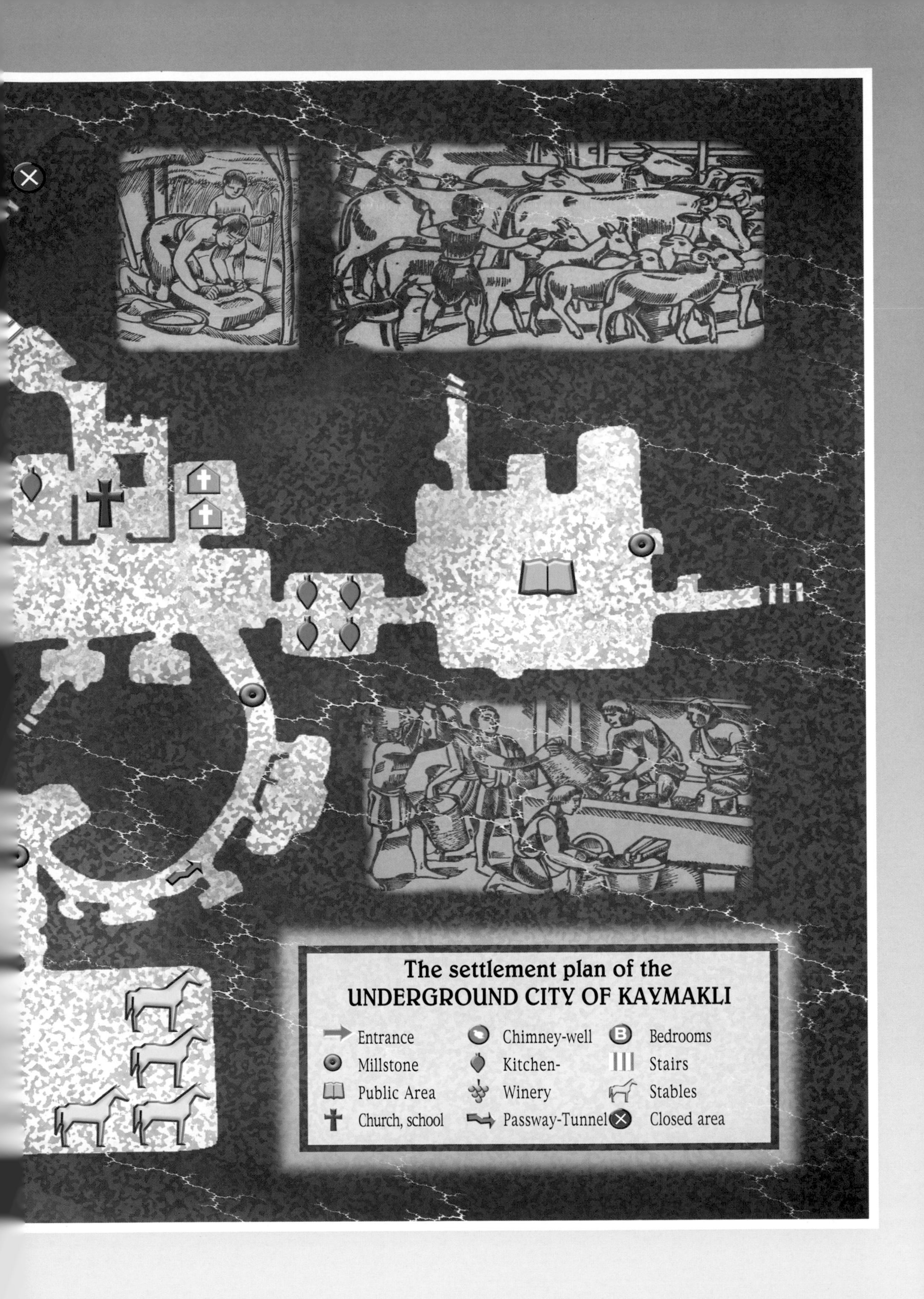
The settlement plan of the
UNDERGROUND CITY OF KAYMAKLI
Entrance
Millstone
Public Area
Church, school
Chimney-well
Kitchen-
Winery
Passway-Tunnel
Bedrooms
Stairs
Stables
Closed area

Toilets of the underground city of Tatlarin (top).
Interiors of the underground city of Saratlı (right).

And again unlike the other underground cities in this area, besides the rolling stone doors, there were holes above the tunnels used for dumping hot oil on the enemy. Similar to Kaymakli and Derinkuyu, Ozkonak has a ventilation system, a water well, a winery and rolling stone doors.

Saratlı

The town of Saratlı is in Gulağaç district that is in the borders of the city of Aksaray. It is 3km from the motorway that connects Aksaray to Nevşehir. It is believed that the first inhabitants moved into town before the spread of Christianity, People who had been nomadic settled in the region during Roman reign.

The underground city which is believed to have seven floors, however only three floors can be seen after the excavations since 1999 as well. The settlement contains storage rooms, wineries, toilet, bathroom, air shafts, stables and long passways like the others is called **Kırkgöz** (Forty eyes) as it has 40 rooms..

Acıgöl-Tatlarin

The oldest dwelling in Acigol, which is on Aksaray-Nevsehir motorway 20 km from Nevsehir is from 8th century BC. Tatlarin is 10 km to Acıgöl District of Nevşehir Province.

The underground city, which is discovered in 1975 but was opened to visiting in 1991, seems to be a monastery complex because of its huge depots, the number of churches. The underground city has spread to very large areas, but only a small part could be cleaned.

The most important feature of the underground city, two floors of which can be visited now, is its having a toilet, which is not found in other underground cities.

Mazı

Mazı Village, whose ancient name was **Mazata**, is 18 km south of Ürgüp and 10 km east of Kaymaklı underground city. Four different entrances could be determined at different locations.

Its main entrance is provided with the corridor made of irregular stones. The large bolt stone in the short corridor takes the entrance and exit of the underground city under control. The small room in the internal side has been made to provide easy movement of the bolt stone.

*U*nderground cities that have not been used for centuries became filled with soil and pieces of rocks carried there by snow and rain waters. The doors and chimneys are blocked and some sections are partially or totally closed. Therefore, people built villages and towns on top of them without noticing the old underground dwelling sometimes.

German scientist Martin Urban, who was the first to extensively research in the area in 1960's, dates the cities from the 7th and 8th centuries B.C..

It is believed that Seljuks also made use of the underground dwellings for military purposes as well, because the dwellings are 5-10km from the Caravanserais.

Different views from Soğanlı Canyon (left) and the interior of the Karabaş Church (top).

SOĞANLI CANYON

Soğanlı is 25km south east of Derinkuyu, 25km east of Yesilhisar and it is 5 km after leaving Yesilhisar-Urgup road. Mavrucan region that is in the middle of the arch extending from Erciyes to Ihlara is in the town of Guzeloz with its modern name.

The canyon is approximately 25km and it is one of the areas examined by R.P. Guillaume de Jerphanion. Different from Urgup and Goreme, both sides of the valley are surrounded by upright Trakyt walls that are 60 degrees to the ground. It is similar to Selime, Yaprakhisar and Ihlara. The trakyt and basalt rock massives that are formed on a thick tuff layer are cracked as a result of the movements of the earth and the water collapsed the sides of it in time, and what we see in the area appeared as a result. Thousands of tomb rooms and mummy cases from Roman and Byzantine time are perplexing to the visitors.

There are 50 churches and monasteries in different sizes in Soganli valley most of which are from

The St. Barbara Church (top) and one of the paintings of the church. The Benediction(detail) (left).

the period between 9th and 13th century. The most important ones are St.Barbara Church, Karabas Church, Buyuk Church, Saint John Church, Yilanli Church, Tokali Church, Saint George Church, and Kubbeli Church.

Kubbeli Church was built carving inside and outside of the rock that is a different technique than the ones used for the others. It is like a tower over-looking the valley. The wild and enchanted of view of the valley brings you to a different time making you feel like even the closest thing in your view extends into eternity.

The Castle of Nevşehir (top).
The Altıkapı Tomb in Ürgüp (right).

NEVŞEHİR

The city was founded by Phrygians. Persians and Macedonians turned it into a capital. After Romans and Byzantines, Seljuk Turks took control of the city after the year 1071. Sejuks actually called the city **Mushkara**. The altitude of the city is between 500-1000m and most of the geological and historical wonders that we have mentioned in this book such as unique valleys, fairy chimneys, rockdwelling churches, underground cities, open air museums are in the borders of this city. The region looks more like it actually belongs to a different planet other than Earth. The major historical monuments are, the castle, Kaya Mosque and Kurşunlu Mosque.

*T*he caravan roads were used by the old civilizations of Anatolia as well as Hittites. They are mentioned in the famous book of **Ksenophon** called **Anabasis** and **Geography** by Strabon. Alexander the Great, the Romans, Saint Paul, and even the troops of the Crusades used these roads. In middle ages, Seljuks founded army bases, Caravanserais, and small castles on their borders, based on what they had learned from Hittites and Romans. They provided safe roads for the transportation of the riches of the east to the west via Anatolia. Nowadays, railways that connect the west of the Anatolia with the east are also parallel to the old trade ways. All of these roads constitute the **Anatolian Silk Road.**

THE SILK ROAD

Views from the Sultan Han Carawanserai.

The transportation of silk and spice, as well as other products of the east, in caravans to the west created the **Silk Road** trade ways that extended from China to Europe. The Silk Road actually crossed Anatolia from one side to the other. It not only provided a means to transport commercial goods and people, but also the opportunity for the exchange of culture between the east and the west.

The west entrances of the Silk Road to Anatolia were two routes. The first route was to the Nikomedia (Izmit) port via the Bosphorus . The second one was to Kyzkos(Bandirma) and Dorylaion (Eskişehir) via the Dardanelles (Çanakkale). The third option was to go to Sardes, the capital of Lydia, via Aegean port cities, like Troy(Truva), Smyrna(Izmir), Ephesus (Efes) and Milotos(Milet).

One of the roads that started from Sardes went to Aparneia(Dinar), while another one was the famous Persian King's Road that eventually reached Caesarea (Kayseri) after arriving in the Hittite's land in northeast direction and crossing over Hallys (Kızılırmak). The road left Kayseri in two different directions. One of them went over the Euphrates River via Malatya and reached the well-known **Transit Road** that connected Anatolia with Asia, having passed through Sivas and Erzurum. The other one joined the road coming from Dinar after Tyana(Bor) in the south and, passing Kilikia, arrived in Adana and the Mediterranean Sea. From Adana, it eventually arrived at Syria. Moreover, it also reached to Europe by seaway using ports such as Trabzon, Sinop, Syria, Antakya, Antalya and Izmir.

During the Seljuks' rule, there were three key elements of trade: roads, caravans, and caravanserais. They symbolized the guarantee of the state over the commercial transportation with their castle-like appearances on the roads, which were in the middle of nowhere, and with their rich stone ornaments and well-planned interior designs.

During the reigns of Kılıçarslan II, and Alaeddin Keykubat I, the number of the caravanserais increased, and security was provided by the Seljuks. There were rooms around the courtyard that were used as bedrooms, kitchens, baths, storage rooms, and toilets. Caravanserais had a couple of different roles. Aside from securing the transportation of goods and travelers, they also created a channel of communication between cultures. They were built 8-10 hours walking distance on foot, or, at most, a day's travel on camel, apart from one another. Research shows us that there were nearly 200 caravanserais in Anatolia, and that they were built 30-40km from each other.

Ağzıkara Han

This is one of the most important carawanserais in Anatolia and it is on the motorway from Aksaray to Nevsehir, 15km from Aksaray. In old times, calligraphers called as **Ağzıkara**, which means **black mouth** in Turkish. When calligraphers were writing their hands would get covered in ink and when they would wet their fingers on their lips before changing pages they would end up with black mouths. The han is very close to Ağzıkara village where there used to be a famous calligrapher, and that is where the name comes from.

The inscriptions on the crown-shaped doors of the han tell us that it began to be built between 1231-1236, during the reign of Allaeddin Keykubat, and that it was completed in 1239, during Gıyaseddin Keyhüsrev's reign. Its monumental crown doors, along with the outside walls that are ornamented with geometrical shapes, are fine examples of the Seljuk art of stone carving.

Sultan Han. A typical decoration sample of the Seljuk stone carving art.

Sultan Han

This carawanserai located on the road connecting Aksaray to Konya, 42 km from Aksaray, was built by the Seljuk Sultan Allaeddin Keykubat in 1229. It is one of the biggest caravanserais in Anatolia, having been built on a 6,120m^2 plot with a courtyard. There are domed arcades on the right of the courtyard opposite to bedrooms and storage rooms. There is a praying room, called **Kiosk-Masjit**, in the middle of the courtyard, which is surrounded by many rooms, a Turkish bath, a bakery and stables. It looks more like a castle with a strong crown door and thick walls supported by towers. It was built by Havlanzade Mehmet who was one of the accomplished Seljuk architects and mason.

The Crown Door of Sarı Han (top).
Ağzıkarahan. A view from courtyard (right).

Today it is very close to its original form, having been renovated.

Sarıhan (Saruhan)

On the road to Ürgüp from Avanos, 25km from Nevşehir and 6km from Avanos. It was estimated to have been built during the time of İzzettin Keykavus on a 2,000m^2 plot of land. It was built with yellow, reddish-yellow, pink and light brown stone blocks that were cut into regular shapes. The arches of the doors were built with stones of two different colors, which gave the doors a distinct look. It is a typical Sultan Carawanserai with a summer section that has a square courtyard and a covered, rectangular winter section. Renovations were completed in 1999.

Pottery and earthenware making is the symbol of Avanos. In the past, donkeys and horses were used to transport the potters to the markets in different cities. There is even a saying about the times when these animals fell down and their cargo was broken into pieces. "Even the blind can find the way to Avanos from the broken pieces of pottery on the road". Today, the red soil carried by Kizilirmak is kept in special wells a couple of years before it is ready to be put on the wheel to make pottery. In approximately 300 hundred workshops, besides seeing the subtle details of the art of making pottery while skilled world famous artisans are working on the wheel, you can actually try turning the wheel yourself.

Views from Avanos. The Cafer Ağa Residence (top). The "Hair Museum of potter Galip(top left).
A potter with his paddle wheel (down left).

Avanos

If you drive 15km from Nevşehir towards north-east, you would reach Avanos by Kizilirmak River having passed through Zelve. Kizilirmak that was the cradle for many civilizations in Anatolia has also given life to Avanos. The name of the region was **Nenessa** in Assyrian trade documents. Hittite archives refer to the area with the name **Zu-Winassa**. In 1st c. BC in Cappadocia language which originated from the Luwi language, Winassa meant empress. Strabon spells the name as **Ouenesa** and mentions that the area is famous for Zeus temple. There is not a city or town under this name. This was the name for the area that also includes the modern town of Avanos. The name was changed into **Vanesa** in sources from Byzantine and early Christianity period. The region got more important with the new faith of the time Christianity and in 7th century a big number of people settled in the area to escape from oppression. The underground city in **Özkonak** which is in the borders of the town of Avanos is one such dwelling. As a result, Venasa became a significant religious center.

Avanos is also famous for hand-made carpets. The little girls learn how to write history with knots from their mums at an early age. You can also witness the process of weaving a carpet. The art of making carpets is passed from generation to generation.

The ruins of the Açıksaray Monastery.

Gülşehir and Açıksaray

It is on the northeast of Nevşehir, on the sides of Kepez Tcpe. Although it is not known when and by whom it is founded, the artifacts found in **Civelek Cave** in the north are from 7500-8000 BC. Monuments from Hittites who inhabited the place 3000-2000 BC, Büyük Kale and Küçük Kale (senior and junior castle) inhabitances, Ovaören (Town of Sivasa) and Gökçetoprak Village are open to public.

The Byzantine name of the dwelling was **Zoropassos**. The name was changed by Seljuks into Arapsun and the dwelling has been called Arapsun until recently. Civelek cave which is km away from Gulsehir is the oldest underground inhabitance of the area. The entrance to the cave that is situated on a hill called Gürlek Hill through a 14 m gallery that goes down in the hill.

In Açıksaray which is on Nevşehir-Gülşehir road, there are underground inhabitances that take up 1km2 of space. In Gülşehir, there are underground cities called Sivasa, Sıgırlı, and Göresin, but they are not open to public.

The St.Jean church is located at the entrance of Gülşehir. It has 2 floors with a barrel-vault and cross design. It is affiliated with a famous monastery complex that is dated to 7th century. In the lower floor

"The Last supper" (top)
and a detail from "Ressurection" (below).

there are wine cellar, water canals and graves. The upper floor is the church and its walls are ornamented with scenes taken from the Bible. The scenes are painted in frieses. On the western and southern walls, the Last Jurisdiction scene, which is rarely seen in Cappadocia Region is used. In accordance with the inscription on the Church abscise; the church is dated to the year 1212. Yellow orange red and brown colors are used to depict Bible stories, which is not very typical in the region.

Scenes are : The Deisis, the Descent from the cross, the Entombment, the Last supper, The Betrayal of Judas and the Baptism.

The prehistoric remains on its banks go back to 3,000 B.C.. It is the longest river in Turkey. It carries the fertile land that it has flowed through for kilometers to the pottery makers in Avanos. The fortune-tellers of King Kroisos of Lydia told him that it would be the end of the existence of a country if he tried to pass Kızılırmak (called Hallys in ancient times). They were right; the King lost his own kingdom. What do you think was the message that Hallys gave to the rich and greedy Kroisos 2,500 years ago? Hallys had been flowing there, giving life to its surroundings, for millions of years before Kroises, or any other human being, came to its banks.

Kızılırmak

The river Kızılırmak (Hallys) begins on the south side of the Kızıldag, which is in the northeastern part of the Middle Anatolia region. It comes from the city Sivas, the ancient name of which is Sebasteia. It flows through numerous villages and towns with bridges and, after 1,355km, reaches the Black Sea in the town of Bafra.

In 2,000 B.C., Hittites who inhabited in the area founded the first known state of Anatolia and, moreover, after the battle of Kadesh, they signed the first written treaty of humankind with Ramses II, the king of Egypt. There were many others, like Phrygians with their rich king Midas who was able to turn everything he touched into gold, and Macedonians, Persians, Cappadocian Kingdom, Romans, Byzantines, Seljuks, and the Ottomans. The river saw the control of many empires with proud kings, many natural disasters and destructions. It witnessed the pompous march of Alexander the Great, Timur and Keyhusrev on their horses with their shiny armies following them. It saw soldiers being killed, kingdoms falling into pieces and the devastation caused by wars and earthquakes. The river knew that civilizations, like living creatures, turned into nothing but dust. Humankind never left after it first came near to the fertile banks of the river and saw its reflection on the surface of the water.

To travel alongside the Kızılırmak means to travel a 1,355 km journey, most of which would be in the Middle Anatolia region. Their distant villages and towns would be alike, in that they were all founded on the bending waters of the river, which has numerous stone tombs on its sides. **Strabon** mentions that the river **Hallys** got the name as it was flowing near the Hallais, which means saltpans in the ancient language. Its waters are a little bitter in taste as a result of the salt. The soft rocks have gypsum and clay that wear away easily and get carried along as the Kızılırmak flows through Mazaka of the Hittites, Kaisareia of the Romans, and Kayseri of modern Turkey.

Views from Kızılırmak.

The river comes into the south end of the big arch it creates in the town of Avanos, then flows into the country of Hacibaktasi Veli, who was said that all humans were brothers and sisters and that God and the people are one. When the river comes close to Lake Tuz, it turns towards north Anatolia, specifically towards the Black Sea next, literally signing the country. Saying farewell to the Ikiztepe of the **Hatti** Kingdom, it flows in to Black Sea in the town of Bafra.

Tuz Gölü (Salt Lake)

Salt Lake is in the Middle Anatolia region in the northeast of the lowest part of the land surrounded by Kizilirmak in the east, Obruk plateau in the south, Cihanbeyli plateau in the west and Haymana plateau in the north. It is the second biggest lake in Anatolia after Lake Van. The lake, which is tectonic geologically, has a closed basin. Although it is the second biggest lake, it is very shallow. In most places it is not deeper than 0.5 meters. During the spring months when water is ample, it gets as big as 164,200 hectares. The area has the driest weather in Turkey, and because it does not often rain it is not rich in rivers. Water sources include the Baglica and Kirdelik streams from the south, Esmekaya spring, Insuyu stream from the west and Pecenek stream from east. However, almost all of these sources dry up before reaching the lake in the summer. Nearly the whole lake desiccates during the summer as a result of extreme evaporation. In dry parts, a layer of salt in 30-centimeter thick is formed. It is one of the saltiest lakes in the world, as well as in Turkey. The density of the water is 1.225 g/cm3, and the percentage of salt in the water is 32.4%. Most of Turkey's salt is obtained from here. It is one of the riches areas of Turkey in terms of the number of birds.

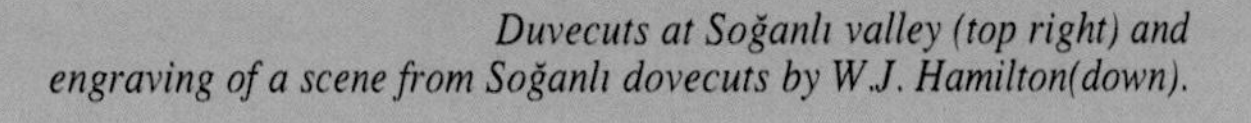

Duvecuts at Soğanlı valley (top right) and engraving of a scene from Soğanlı dovecuts by W.J. Hamilton(down).

Dovecuts of Cappadocia

It is known that raising pigeons in Anatolia is a very old tradition dating back to 3000BC. Pigeons have always been considered sacred in this region. Moreover, they were very helpful to the people of Anatolia as a means of communication especially in the deserted or scarcely populated parts of Anatolia. Charles Texier and William Hamilton who visited Cappadocia at the beginning of the 18th century attracted attention to these birds in their travel notes and drawings. We can see thousands of examples of these dovecuts in Ürgüp-Üzengire valley, Ortahisar, Balkan Deresi, Kızılçukur valley, Kiliclar and Güllüdere valleys, valleys around Uçhisar. You can see them among the houses, churches and monasteries carved into the rock.

Cappadocia is where grape is grown in Middle Anatolia. To get better harvest from the grapevines have required the farmers to use pigeon excrement as fertilizers, and therefore many dovecuts were built, that is carved in the tufa rocks around the grapevines. Here the secret of growing good grapes is the pigeons and tufa. When the dovecuts are built variables like the water sources around, the amount of sunshine that the inside of the houses get and the side of a mountain that they would be put is considered. There are very small holes as entries for pigeons and the outside walls of the rooms are covered with limestone and egg white that hardens very fast and gets so slippery that it is harder for other wild animals to climb up the rooms. The sides of the pigeon houses are decorated with animal and plant motifs that reflect traditions and personal taste traditional kilim (some sort of a rock) patterns that are traditional. These also attract the attention of the birds.

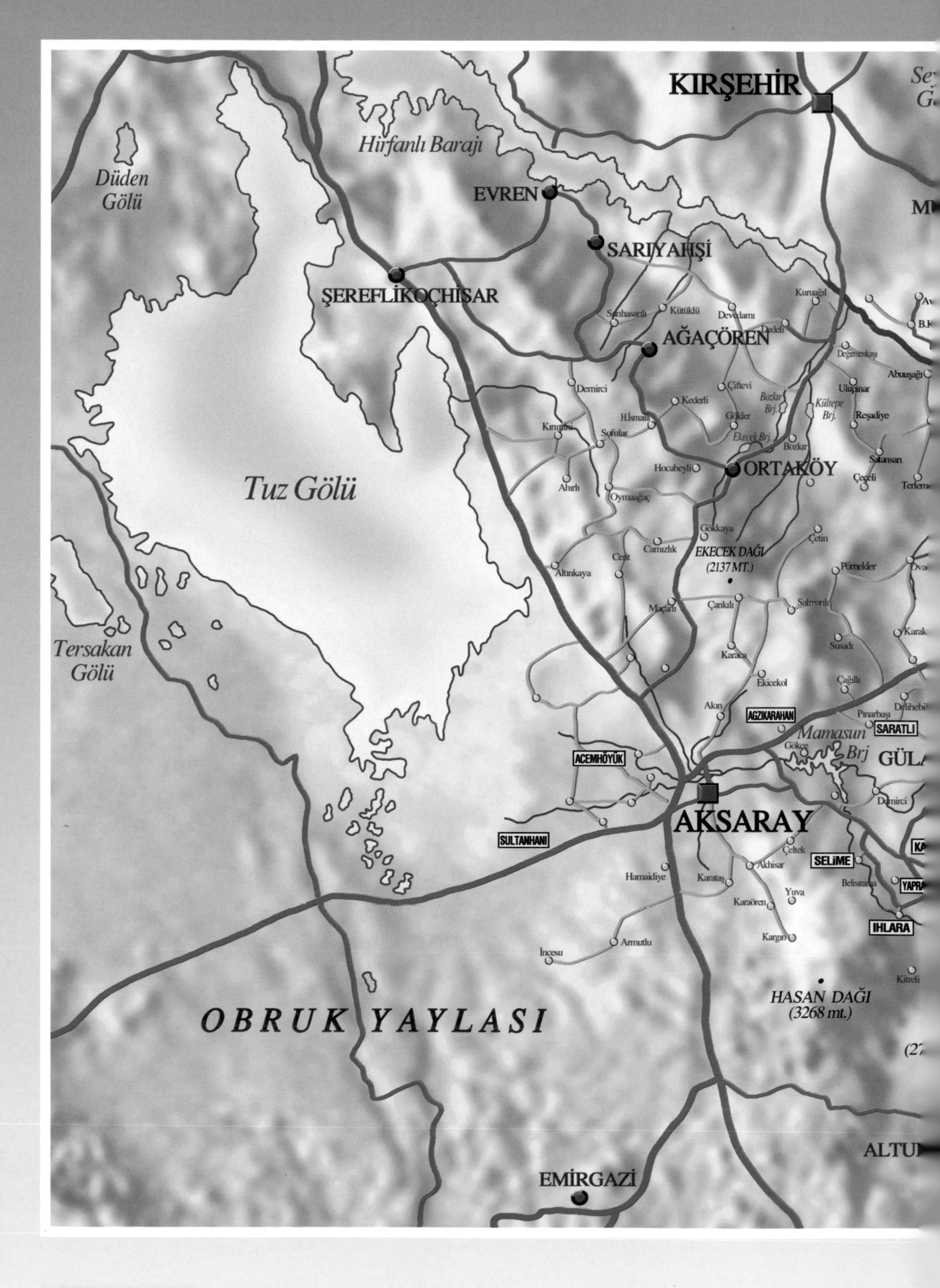
KIRŞEHİR
Hirfanlı Baraji
Düden Gölü
EVREN
SARIYAHŞİ
ŞEREFLİKOÇHİSAR
AĞAÇÖREN
Kuruağıl
Şahhasanlı
Kütüklü
Devedamı
Dadeli
Değirmenkaşı
Abuuşağı
Demirci
Çiftevi
Ulupınar
Kederli
Bozkır Brj.
Kültepe Brj.
Reşadiye
H.İsmailli
Gökler
Kırımlını
Sofular
Ekecek Brj.
Bozkır
Sılansan
Hocabeyli
ORTAKÖY
Çeçeli
Ahırlı
Tuz Gölü
Oymaağaç
Gökkaya
Çetin
Camızlık
EKECEK DAĞI
(2137 MT.)
Cerit
Altınkaya
Pömekler
Maçanlı
Çankılı
Salmanlı
Tersakan Gölü
Susadı
Karaca
Ekicekol
Çağıllı
Akın
AGZIKARAHAN
Pınarbaşı
Mamasun Brj
SARATLI
Gökçe
ACEMHÖYÜK
Demirci
AKSARAY
SULTANHANI
Çeltek
SELİME
Hamaidiye
Akhisar
Kurataş
Yuva
Belisırama
Karaören
IHLARA
Kargın
Armutlu
İncesu
Kitreli
HASAN DAĞI
(3268 mt.)
OBRUK YAYLASI
EMİRGAZİ

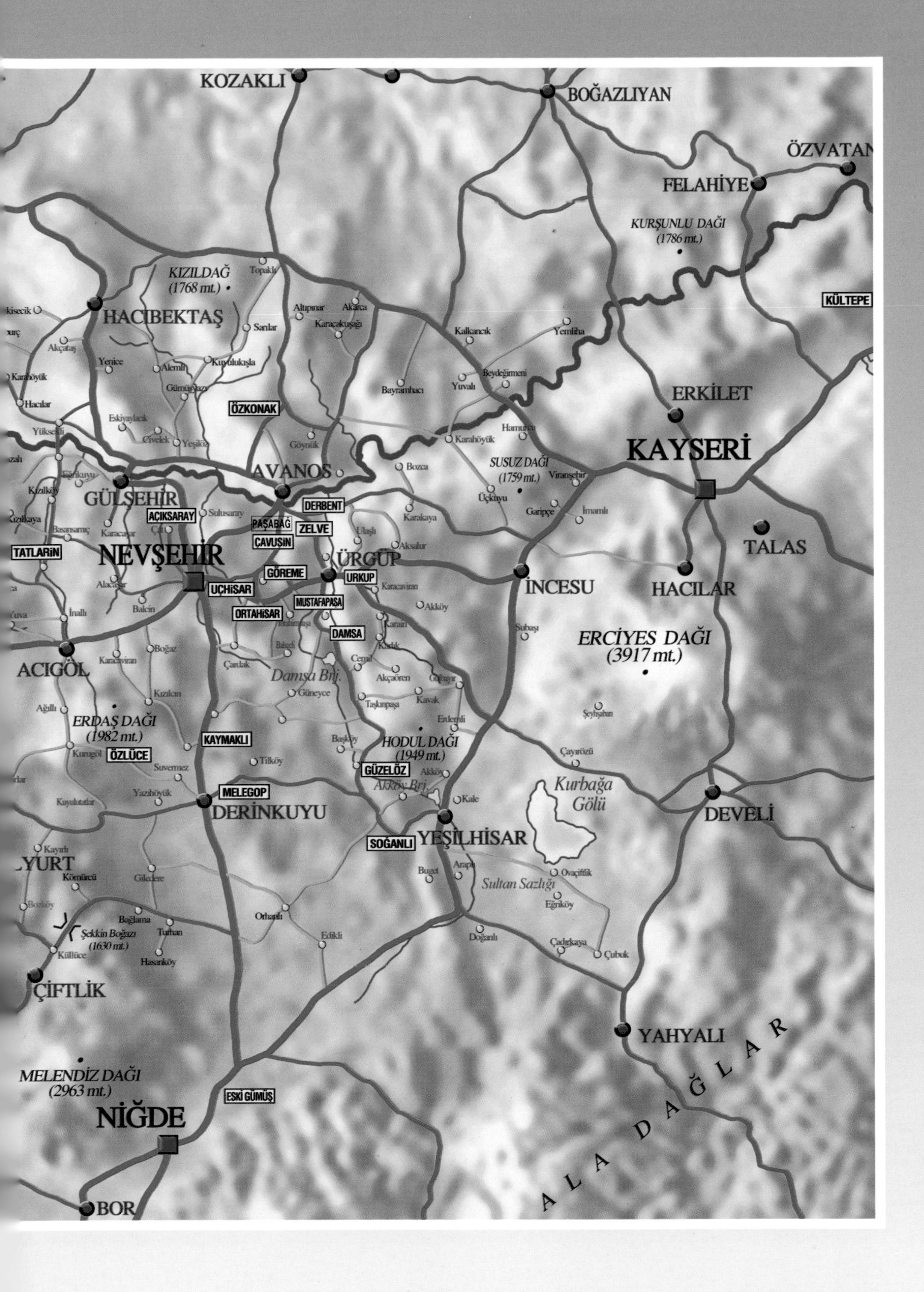

KOZAKLI
BOĞAZLIYAN
ÖZVATAN
FELAHİYE
KURŞUNLU DAĞI
(1786 mt.)
KÜLTEPE
KIZILDAĞ
(1768 mt.)
Topaklı
HACIBEKTAŞ
Sarılar
Altıpınar
Akarca
Karacakuşağı
Kalkancık
Yemliha
Akçataş
Yenice
Alemli
Kuyulukışla
Gümüşyazı
Bayramhacı
Yuvalı
Beydeğirmeni
Hacılar
ÖZKONAK
ERKİLET
Eskiyaylacık
Çivelek
Yeşilöz
Göynük
Hamurcu
Karahöyük
KAYSERİ
AVANOS
Bozca
SUSUZ DAĞI
(1759 mt.)
Viranşehir
Kızılköy
GÜLŞEHİR
Sulusaray
DERBENT
Üçkuyu
Garipçe
İmamlı
AÇIKSARAY
Kızılkaya
Karacaşar
PAŞABAĞ
ZELVE
Karakaya
TALAS
Ulaşlı
ÇAVUŞİN
Aksalur
TATLARİN
NEVŞEHİR
ÜRGÜP
GÖREME
URKUP
İNCESU
HACILAR
UÇHİSAR
Karacaviran
MUSTAFAPAŞA
Akköy
Balcin
ORTAHİSAR
İnallı
DAMSA
Subaşı
ERCİYES DAĞI
(3917 mt.)
Boğaz
Bahçeli
Karain
ACIGÖL
Karacaviran
Çardak
Cemil
Damsa Brj.
Akçaören
Gülbayır
Güneyce
Ağıllı
Kızılcın
Taşkınpaşa
Kavak
Şeyhşaban
ERDAŞ DAĞI
(1982 mt.)
Erdemli
KAYMAKLI
Başköy
HODUL DAĞI
(1949 mt.)
Kurugöl
ÖZLÜCE
Tilköy
Çayırözü
Suvermez
GÜZELÖZ
Akköy
Kurbağa Gölü
Akköy Brj.
Yazıhöyük
MELEGOP
Kale
Kuyulutatlar
DERİNKUYU
DEVELİ
SOĞANLI
YEŞİLHİSAR
Kayırlı
YURT
Kömürcü
Giledere
Buget
Arapli
Ovaçiftlik
Sultan Sazlığı
Bozköy
Eğriköy
Bağlama
Orhanlı
Şekkin Boğazı
(1630 mt.)
Turhan
Edikli
Doğanlı
Çadırkaya
Çubuk
Küllüce
Hasanköy
ÇİFTLİK
YAHYALI
MELENDİZ DAĞI
(2963 mt.)
ESKİ GÜMÜŞ
NİĞDE
ALA DAĞLAR
BOR

BIBLIOGRAPHY

AKŞİT İlhan, Hititler, Sandoz Yayınları, İstanbul, 1981
AKTÜRE Sevgi, Anadolu'da Bronz Çağı Kentleri, Tarih Vakfı Yurt Yayınları, İstanbul, 1994
AKURGAL Ekrem, Anadolu Kültür Tarihi, Tübitak Popüler Bilim Kitapları, Ankara,1998
AKURGAL Ekrem, Anadolu Uygarlıkları , Net Turistik Yayınlar , İstanbul , 1989
AKURGAL Ekrem , Hatti Uygarlığı, Remzi Oğuz Arık Armağanı, Ankara Üniversitesi Dil ve Tarih-Coğrafya Fakültesi Yayınları, Ankara, 1987
AKYILDIZ Erhan, Taş Çağı'ndan Osmanlı'ya Anadolu, Milliyet Yayınları, İstanbul, 1984
ALKIM Bahadır, Anatolia I,Form the Beginnigs to the end of the 2nd Millenium BC, Nagel Publishers, Geneva, 1970
ALP Sedat, Hitit Çağında Anadolu, Tübitak Popüler Bilim Kitapları, Ankara, 2001
ARIK Remzi Oğuz, Les Fouilles d'Alacahöyük 1935, Türk Tarih Kurumu Yayınları, Ankara,1937
ARIKAN Yasemin, Hitit Dini Üzerine Bir İnceleme, Ankara Üniversitesi Dil ve Tarih-Coğrafya Fakültesi Dergisi Cilt 38 Sayı 1-2,
BAŞDEMİR Kürşat, Eski Anadolu, Tarihsel ve Kültürel Süreklilik, Kaynak Yayınları, İstanbul, 1999
CERAM C.W., Tanrıların Vatanı Anadolu, Remzi Kitabevi, İstanbul, 1979
ÇIĞ Muazzez İlmiye, Hititler ve Hattuşa, Kaynak Yayınları, İstanbul, 2000
DARGA Muhibbe, Hitit Sanatı, Akbank Kültür ve Sanat Kitapları, İstanbul, 1992
ERTEM Hayri, Boğazköy Metinlerinde Geçen Coğrafya Adları Dizini, Ankara Üniversitesi Dil ve Tarih-Coğrafya Fakültesi Yayınları, Ankara 1973
ERTEM Hayri, Hitit Devletinin İki Eyaleti: Pala - Tum(m)ana, Ankara Üniversitesi Dil ve Tarih-Coğrafya Fakültesi Yayınları, Ankara 1980
EYUBOĞLU İsmet Zeki, Anadolu Mitolojisi, Toplumsal Dönüşüm Yayınları, İstanbul, 1998EYUBOĞLU İsmet Zeki, Anadolu Uygarlığı , Der Yayınları, İstanbul, 1981
GIBBON Edward, Roma İmparatorluğu ,/ Bilim, Felsefe, Sanat Yayınları İstanbul,
GUERNEY O.R. , The Hittites, Penguin Books , Middlesex , 1990 (Türkçesi : Hititler, çev. Pınar Arpaçay, Dost Kitabevi, Ankara,2001)
İNCİL Yohanna, Matta ve Luca / Kitab-ı Mukaddes ayınları, İstanbul.
KINAL Fürüzan , Eski Anadolu Tarihi , Türk Tarih Kurumu Yayınları , Ankara , 1987
LLOYD Seton, Türkiye'nin Tarihi, Bir Gezginin Gözüyle Anadolu Uygarlıkları, Tübitak Popüler Bilim Kitapları, Ankara,1997
LLOYD Seton, Early Anatolia, Penguin Books , Middlesex,1956
MACQUEEN J.G. , The Hittites and Their Contemporaries in Asia Minor , Thames and Hudson, London, 1986
OHRİ İskender, Anadolu'nun Öyküsü, Milliyet Yayınları, İstanbul, 1983
SAVAŞ Savaş Özkan, Anadolu (Hitit-Luvi) Hiyeroglif Yazıtlarında Geçen Tanrı,Şahıs ve Coğrafya Adları, Ege Yayınları, İstanbul, 1998
SEVİN Veli, Anadolu Arkeolojisinin ABC'si, Simavi Yayınları, İstanbul,1991
TUNA Celâl, Mağaradan Kente, Anadolu'nun En Eski Yerleşim Yerleri, İletişim Yayınları, İstanbul, 2000
ÜNAL Ahmet, Boğazköy Metinleri Işığında Hititler Devri Anadolu'sunda Filolojik ve Arkeolojik Veriler arasındaki İlişkilerden Örnekler, 1992 Yılı Anadolu Medeniyetleri Müzesi Konferansları, Anadolu Medeniyetleri Müzesini Koruma ve Yaşatma Derneği Yayını, Ankara 1993
ALP Sedat, Hitit Çağında Anadolu, Tübitak Popüler Bilim Kitapları, Ankara, 2001
ERHAT Azra , Mitoloji Sözlüğü , Remzi Kitabevi, İstanbul, 1978
HERODOTOS, Herodot Tarihi (çev. Müntekim Ökmen), Remzi Kitabevi, İstanbul, 1973
SEVİN Veli, Frygler, Anadolu Uygarlıkları Görsel Anadolu Tarihi Ansiklopedisi, Görsel Yayınlar, İstanbul, 1982
STRABON , Coğrafya / Anadolu, Kitap: XII, XIII, XIV (çev:Adnan Pekman), Arkeoloji ve Sanat Yayınları , İstanbul, 1987
UMAR Bilge, Türkiye'deki Tarihsel Adlar /İnkılap Yayınları, İstanbul, 1993

Prepared By:

Author: Jeoffrey LAMEC
Art Selection and Design: Melih ÖNDÜN
Photographs: Erdal YAZICI
Translation: Ramazan GÜNGÖR
Colour Separation and Films: 3 B Grafik
Printing: Ebat Basım A.Ş.

Cappadocia, Istanbul 2006

ISBN 975 -7499 -25 -0

SILK ROAD TOURISTIC PUBLICATIONS
General Yazgan Sok. No: 13/3 Tünel, İstanbul - TURKEY
Tel: 0212-245 31 41 Fax: 0212-245 75 83